~ The Candy Bar Cookbook ~

❧ The Candy Bar Cookbook ❧

Baking with America's Favorite Candy

BY ALISON INCHES & RIC MCKOWN

PHOTOGRAPHS BY ANN CHANDLER BROWN

ILLUSTRATIONS BY ALEXANDRA FOLEY

LONGSTREET PRESS
Atlanta, Georgia

Published by
LONGSTREET PRESS
2140 Newmarket Parkway
Suite 122
Marietta, GA 30067

Printed in Mexico

ISBN: 1-56352-609-3

᪥ FOR OUR DADS ᪥

ACKNOWLEDGMENTS

Special thanks to Rob Robertson, Ann Brown, Michael Taylor
Alexandra Foley, Tysie Whitman and Sally Hoagland.

❧

We would also like to thank the following friends and Wednesday Night Dessert Club taste-testers: Peter Allen, Shellie Batten, Doug and Ann Brown, Doug Burns, Deborah Clark, Jean Duperrault, Chris Eddington, Margie Foerster, Paul Goodrich, Cindy Glick, Linda Hambrick, Lisa Hambrick, Christy Hoerner, KT, Ken, Kris, and Kevin Hom, Barbara Hurwick, Joanie and Henny Inches, Jim Linlor, the Los Gatos Volleyball Crew, Kevin and Liz Massey, Rosemary Metz, Bob McDowell, Bill and Kathy McKown, Wendy Remington, Tracie Reynolds, Susan and Neal Sebbard, Fleurette Sevin, Alan Wiersba, Pamela Whitenack, Pete and Liz Williams, Mary Wills, Heather Wilson, Susan and Christopher Wright.

∾ The Candy Bar Cookbook ∾

Table of Contents

Introduction

The corner store where I grew up was called DeFazio's. Mrs. DeFazio had gray hair swirled like a breakfast danish on top of her head. She wore sturdy black shoes on her feet, glasses on a chain and a permanent frown on her face. She would straighten ketchup bottles and rearrange cereal boxes as I studied the candy rack. I struggled to narrow it down to a Hershey's® Milk Chocolate Bar every time. When I was big enough, my friends and I rode bikes to The Dandelion, a new candy store on the block. Our kickstands clicked one by one as we parked our bikes under the bobbing balloons outside the door. John, the owner, still knows me by name. He stocked everything from candy bars to Pixie® Sticks, Atomic Fire Balls®, Smarties®, Root Beer Barrels®, Wax Lips® and Whoppers®. He gave us colored baskets to hold the candy when our fists got too full. Whistling songs like a spring warbler, he rang up our purchases and dropped them into tiny brown bags. We peddled to the playground, clutching our candy loot against the handlebars.

My candy trail soon led to my husband, Ric McKown. When Ric and I began dating, he owned a bakery in Mountain View, California. One day, I asked him if he wanted to combine my love of candy with his love of baking in a cookbook. The combination was so good, we decided to get married *and* create *The Candy Bar Cookbook*.

Candy bars have achieved a rare status shared by vintage lunchboxes, Superman comic books, Coca Cola® and roadside tourist attractions—a pop culture phenomenon we've all come to know as Americana. *The Candy Bar Cookbook* is for those of us who know the delightful lure of chocolate bars in nostalgic wrappers, gum drops in rectangular boxes, and twisted licorice ropes in cellophane. This cookbook is a tribute to over 100 years of candy making in America.

We hope you enjoy it as much as we enjoyed making it for you.

Bon Bon Appetit!
—Alison Inches

Food for thought: We highly recommend removing the candy wrappers before preparing the following recipes...

Candy Bar Time Line

1800's Circus Peanuts • Marshmallows first manufactured in the U.S.

1847 The Candy Cane comes to America

1852 Ghirardelli® Chocolate Company founded

1893 Good & Plenty® • Good & Fruity® • Juicy Fruit® Gum • Wrigley's® Spearmint Gum

1894 Hershey's® Milk Chocolate Bar • Hershey's® Milk Chocolate with Almonds • Cella's®

1896 Cracker Jack® • Tootsie Roll®

1890's Dots® • Crows® (originally Black Crows®)

1902 Animal Crackers® • Sweethearts® Brand Conversation Hearts

1904 Ice Cream Cones invented

1907 Hershey's® Kisses®

1912 Necco® Wafers • Goo Goo Clusters® • Mountain Bar® (originally Mount Tacoma Bar®)

1914 Mary Jane®

1916 Butternut® Bar

1917 Clark® Bar • Charms® Squares

1918 Life Savers® • Goetze's® Caramel Creams

1919 Nestlé® Milk Chocolate Bar • Nestlé® Chocolate with Almonds

1920's Sno Caps® • U-No® • Abba Zaba® • Fannie May® Candies opens

1920 Oh Henry!® • Baby Ruth® • Jujyfruits® • Zero® • Mounds®

1921 Chuckles® • See's Famous Old Time Candies®

1922 Charleston Chew!®

1923 Milky Way® • Almond Roca® Buttercrunch

1924 Bit-O-Honey®

1925 Mr. Goodbar® • Goobers® • Sugar Daddy® (originally Papa Sucker®) • Red Vines®

1926 Milk Duds® • Butterfinger®

1927 Raisinets® • Milk Shake® Bar

1928 Heath® Bar

1930's Red Hots® • Boston Baked Beans® • Chunky® • Valomilk® Bar

1930 Snickers® • Zagnut®

1931 Tootsie Pops®

1932 3 Musketeers® • Pay Day®

1933 Nestlé® Toll House® Cookies invented by Ruth Wakefield

1935 Sugar Babies®

1936 Mars Bar® • 5th Avenue®

1937 Sky Bar® • Hershey's® Bittersweet Bar

1938 Krackel® Bar • Nestlé Crunch®

1939 Hershey's® Assorted Miniatures™ • Whoppers® (originally Giants®)

1940 York® Peppermint Patties • Mike and Ike®

1941 M&M's® • Reese's® Peanut Butter Cups®

1946 Almond Joy®	**1982** Skor®
1947 Bazooka® Bubblegum	**1989** Symphony® Creamy Milk Chocolate • Symphony® Creamy Milk Chocolate with Almonds & Toffee Chips
1948 Pom Poms®	
1949 Junior Mints® • Jolly Ranchers® • Hershey's® Semi-Sweet Bar • Smarties® • El Bubble® Gum Cigars	**1990** Hershey's® Kisses® with Almonds • Cherri and Bubb®
1950's Charms® Pops • Andes® Candies • Rocky Road® • Big Hunk® • Look®	**1990's** M&M's® Peanut Butter • M&M's® Almond • Hershey's® Kisses® with Almonds
1950 Hot Tamales® • Topps® Trading Cards • Pez® introduced to American market	**1992** Dove® Promises® • Mega Warheads®
1954 M&M's® Peanut • Marshmallow Peeps® • Atomic Fireballs®	**1993** Nutrageous® • Hershey's® Hugs® • Super Hot Tamales®
1960 Blammo® Bubblegum	**1994** Hershey's® Cookies 'n' Mint Nuggets™ • Fluffy Stuff® Cotton Candy
1962 Now and Later® • After Eight® • Lemonhead®	**1995** M&M's® Mini Chocolate Baking Bits • Blue M&M's® added to mix • Hershey's® Cookies 'n' Crème • Lavender Marshmallow Peeps® • Sidewalk Chalk® Bubblegum
1964 Root-T-Toots®	
1965 Caravelle®	
1966 100 Grand® • Jolly Joes®	**1996** Scharffen Berger® Chocolate Maker founded • M&M's® Minis • Hershey's® Cookies 'n' Crème Nuggets™ • Mike and Ike® Tropical Fruit • Caramel Apple Pops®
1968 Charms® Blow Pop	
1970's Pop Rocks® • Zip-A-Dee-Doo-Das®	
1971 Special Dark® • Rolos® introduced to American market	**1997** Reese's Crunchy Cookie Cups® • Mike and Ike® Berry Fruits
1973 Kit Kat® introduced to American market	**1998** ReeseSticks® • Hershey's® Nuggets Creamy Milk Chocolate with Toffee and Almonds • Hershey's® Nuggets Dark Chocolate with Almonds • Blue Marshmallow Peeps®
1976 Starburst® Fruit Chews • Reese's Crunchy Peanut Butter Cup® • Jelly Bellys® • Milk Chocolate Mounds®	
1977 Twix® Bars • Teenee Beanees®	**1999** M&M's® Crispy • Hershey's® Bites® • Bizzerks® • S'Moresels®
1978 Watchamacallit® • Reese's Pieces®	
1979 Milky Way® Dark • Big League Chew®	**2000** Mocha Crunch® • York® Chocolate Covered Peppermint Bites™ • Nestlé® Yogurt Raisinets® • Super Tootsie Pop® • Winter Clark® • Sour Skittles®
1980's Bubble Tape® • OUCH!® Bubblegum • Gummy Bears introduced to American market by Goelitz®	

The Cookie Jar Meets the Chocolate Bar

~ Cookies, Bars and Biscotti ~

Oatmeal Cookies with Raisinets®

∾ Classic oatmeal raisin cookies. ∾

DIFFICULTY: 🌢🌢

EQUIPMENT: cookie sheet, electric mixer, small ice cream scoop or teaspoon

FOR THE COOKIES

8 ounces butter (2 sticks), room temperature
¾ cup sugar
¾ cup brown sugar
2 eggs
½ teaspoon vanilla
½ teaspoon orange extract
½ teaspoon ground cinnamon
1¼ cups flour
¼ teaspoon baking soda
½ teaspoon salt
3 cups old-fashioned rolled oats
6 bags of Raisinets® (1.58 oz. bags)

MAKE THE COOKIES

1. Preheat the oven to 350° and spray a cookie sheet with nonstick spray.

2. In a large bowl using electric mixer, cream the butter, sugar, brown sugar, eggs, vanilla, orange extract and cinnamon on medium for 2 minutes, scraping down the sides of the bowl.

3. Add the flour, baking soda, salt and oats. Mix until fully incorporated.

4. Fold in the Raisinets®.

5. Using an ice cream scoop or teaspoon, scoop 1-inch balls of dough onto the prepared cookie sheet, spacing 2 inches apart.

6. Bake 11 to 13 minutes. Let the cookies stand for 2 minutes before transferring to a rack. Makes about 36 cookies.

RAISINETS® AND GOOBERS®

The Blumenthal Chocolate Company of Philadelphia debuted Raisinets® in 1927. Their popular chocolate-covered peanut companion, Goobers®, came out in 1925. The word *goober* has its origin in the African word for peanut. Southerners are also known to call peanuts goobers and this may well stem from African Americans who worked on peanut plantations in the South. The Blumenthals, who trademarked the name, had been Southerners before moving to the Northeast.

Brownies with Reese's® Bites™ and Chocolate Glaze

∽ The best-selling brownie at Ric's bakery, Countrymade. ∽

DIFFICULTY: 🍫🍫🍫
EQUIPMENT: 13 x 9-inch pan, electric mixer, double boiler

FOR THE CHOCOLATE BROWNIE LAYER

4 ounces unsweetened chocolate
6 ounces butter (1½ sticks)
1 cup sugar
½ cup brown sugar
1 egg
½ teaspoon salt
½ teaspoon vanilla
1 cup flour
1½ cups Reese's® Bites™

FOR THE PEANUT BUTTER BROWNIE LAYER

¾ cup creamy peanut butter
6 ounces butter (1½ sticks), room temperature
1 cup sugar
1 cup brown sugar
2 eggs
½ teaspoon salt
½ teaspoon vanilla
1½ cups flour

FOR THE CHOCOLATE GLAZE

1 cup semi-sweet chocolate chips
2 tablespoons butter
5 ounces whipping cream

MAKE THE CHOCOLATE BROWNIE LAYER

1. Preheat the oven to 375° and spray a 13 x 9-inch pan with nonstick spray.

2. In a heavy saucepan over low heat, melt the chocolate and butter together. Stir until smooth. Cool chocolate mixture for 10 minutes.

3. In a medium bowl using electric mixer, cream together sugar, brown sugar, eggs, salt and vanilla on high.

4. Blend in chocolate mixture.

5. Add flour and mix until thoroughly incorporated. Fold in Reese's® Bites.™

6. Spread the batter evenly over the bottom of the pan. Set aside.

continued on page 5

Make the Peanut Butter Brownie Layer

1. In a medium bowl using electric mixer, cream together peanut butter and butter.

2. Mix in the sugar, brown sugar, eggs, salt and vanilla. Add the flour and mix until thoroughly incorporated.

3. Spread evenly on top of the chocolate brownie layer.

4. Bake 35 to 40 minutes until golden, or until a toothpick inserted in the middle of the brownies comes out clean. Cool completely before glazing.

Make the Chocolate Glaze

1. In a double boiler over medium heat, melt the chips and butter with one-third of the cream. Remove from heat and stir until smooth.

2. Add the remaining cream and stir until thoroughly incorporated.

3. Pour the glaze on top of the cooled brownies and spread evenly.

4. Cool in the refrigerator for 15 minutes.

5. Cut into 2 x 3-inch squares. Makes 18 to 24 brownies.

REESE'S® PEANUT BUTTER CUPS®

Harry Burnett Reese, an employee of Milton Hershey in the 1920's, had his own dreams of making it big in the candy business. He created candy confections in his kitchen—right down the street from Hershey's chocolate factory. A sugar ration during WWII forced Mr. Reese to seek new ingredients for his candy. He turned to peanut butter and hit the jackpot. Reese's® Peanut Butter Cups® debuted to great success in 1941. Twenty-two years later, Hershey's, the company that inspired Mr. Reese, bought the H. B. Reese Co.

Chocolate Chip Cookies with Hershey's® Assorted Miniatures™

~ A great variation on the traditional chocolate chip cookie. ~

DIFFICULTY: 🌢🌢

EQUIPMENT: cookie sheet, electric mixer, small ice cream scoop or teaspoon

FOR THE COOKIES

45 Hershey's® Assorted Miniatures™
8 ounces butter (2 sticks), room temperature
1 cup sugar
1 cup brown sugar
2 eggs
1 teaspoon vanilla
1 teaspoon baking soda
1 teaspoon salt
3 cups flour

MAKE THE COOKIES

1. Preheat the oven to 325°. Spray a cookie sheet with nonstick spray.

2. Coarsely chop the candy bars.

3. In a large bowl using electric mixer, cream the butter, sugar and brown sugar. Beat in the eggs and vanilla.

4. Add the baking soda, salt and flour and mix until well blended.

5. Fold in the chopped candy bars.

6. Using an ice cream scoop or teaspoon, scoop 1-inch rounds of dough onto prepared cookie sheet 2 inches apart.

7. Bake for 9 to 11 minutes or until just golden.

8. Let rest for 2 minutes before transferring to a rack.

9. Cool completely before storing. Makes about 3 dozen cookies.

HERSHEY'S® ASSORTED MINIATURES™

Hershey's sales reps handed out sample-sized versions of the latest Hershey's® Bar to prospective customers. Customers loved the miniature bars so much that Hershey's began to package and sell them in 1939. The original assortment included Hershey's® Milk Chocolate, Bittersweet®, Aero®, Nougat-Almond® and Krackel®. Today's assortment includes Hershey's® Milk Chocolate, Special Dark®, Krackel® and Mr. Goodbar®.

Scharffen Berger® Brownies

∽ *The best brownies on the planet.* ∽

Contributed by Robert Steinberg, co-founder of Scharffen Berger Chocolate Maker.

DIFFICULTY: 🌶🌶
EQUIPMENT: 8-inch square baking pan, parchment paper (optional), double boiler, whisk

FOR THE BROWNIES

*8 ounces Scharffen Berger® 70% Bittersweet
 Chocolate, chopped*
6 tablespoons butter
¹/₄ teaspoon salt
¹/₂ teaspoon vanilla
1 cup sugar
2 large eggs
¹/₄ cup all-purpose flour
¹/₂ to 1 cup walnuts, optional

MAKE THE BROWNIES

1. Preheat the oven to 325° and lightly butter and flour an 8-inch square baking pan. (We recommend lining the pan with parchment paper.)

2. In a double boiler over medium-low, heat the chocolate and butter. Stir until smooth. Remove from heat and separate the double boiler.

3. Add the salt, vanilla and sugar to the chocolate mixture. Add the eggs one at a time, whisking after addition.

4. Add the flour and whisk for 1 minute until the mixture is shiny and pulls away from the side of the pan.

5. Pour the batter into the prepared pan. Bake for 35 to 40 minutes or until a toothpick inserted in the center of the brownies comes out clean. Cool on a rack. Makes 16 2 x 2-inch brownies.

SCHARFFEN BERGER® CHOCOLATE

When Americans return from Europe, they often talk about the delicious chocolate. When Robert Steinberg returned from Europe in 1994, he became a premier chocolate maker. Formerly a doctor, Robert left his practice and learned the craft of chocolate making in Lyons, France. Together with his business partner John Scharffenberger, a notable California wine maker, they founded Scharffen Berger Chocolate Maker in 1996. Their chocolate is made of a rich blend of hand-picked, well-fermented cocoa beans from places such as Venezuela, Ghana and Papua New Guinea. Even the vintage machinery that roasts and grinds their beans has been imported from Europe. Open a hand-wrapped Scharffen Berger chocolate bar and you will taste a rich mélange of cocoa flavors that simply leaves behind a satisfying trail of MMMMMMMade in the U.S. of A.

M&M's® Meringues

~ A great light treat. ~

DIFFICULTY: 🌢🌢
EQUIPMENT: cookie sheet, electric mixer, small ice cream scoop or teaspoon, parchment paper or brown paper

FOR THE MERINGUES

3 egg whites
¹/₂ teaspoon cream of tartar
³/₄ cup sugar
1¹/₄ cup M&M's® BRAND Mini Baking Bits
 (plus additional for garnish as needed)

MAKE THE MERINGUES

1. Preheat the oven to 275° and line a cookie sheet with a piece of brown or parchment paper. Set aside.

2. In a clean, dry mixing bowl, beat the egg whites and cream of tartar until foamy. While beating, slowly add the sugar and beat until stiff peaks form. Carefully fold in the M&M's®.

3. Using an ice cream scoop or teaspoon, scoop 2-inch round meringues onto the lined cookie sheet about 2 inches apart. (For a festive look, dot the top of each meringue with more M&M's®.)

4. Bake for 1¹/₂ hours.

5. Turn the oven off and leave the meringues inside the closed oven for at least 2 hours—overnight is fine.

6. Transfer to a rack and cool completely. Makes 8 to 10 2-inch meringues.

M&M'S®

The initials "M" and "M" stand for Mars and Murrie, or Forrest Mars Sr. and his partner Bruce Murrie. According to company lore, Mr. Mars got the idea for M&M's® in Spain. On his trip, he met Spanish Civil War soldiers carrying sugarcoated chocolate drops for snacks. The candy shell on the outside of the chocolate intrigued Mr. Mars. He had been looking for a way to keep chocolate from melting so it could be sold year-round. Upon his return in 1941, he invented M&M's®. Now that happy click of candy shells pouring into cupped hands is known all over the world.

M&M'S® URBAN LEGENDS

Many Americans believe that certain color M&M's® have magical properties. The green ones are thought to be aphrodisiacs. A pouch of green M&M's® for a bride-to-be is not uncommon at a lingerie shower. The orange ones have been said to enhance breast size. The brown ones have been rumored to have an adverse affect on the heavy metal band Van Halen. If Van Halen saw a brown M&M® at one of their concerts, the gig was off. The American public had the power to bring the red ones back in 1987 after they had been dropped during the Red Dye No. 2 scare in 1976. And blue ones were voted to replace the tan ones in a nationwide election in 1995.

SUGAR BABIES®

Candy makers Robert and James Welch created a whole family of popular caramel confections that began with the Papa Sucker® in 1925. This caramel lollipop was so large it was considered to be the "big daddy" of all lollipops. It was soon dubbed the Sugar Daddy®. The Sugar Daddy® got a Sugar Mama® in 1935 and Sugar Babies® followed the same year. These chewy caramel children were named after the burlesque dancing girls in the Broadway hit *Sugar Babies*.

Molasses Cookies with Sugar Babies®

∾ Chewy and gingery, Baby! ∾

DIFFICULTY: 🔺🔺

EQUIPMENT: cookie sheet, electric mixer, small ice cream scoop or teaspoon, drinking glass

FOR THE COOKIES

3 cups flour
1 teaspoon baking soda
1/2 teaspoon salt
1 teaspoon ground ginger
1/2 teaspoon ground cloves
1 1/2 teaspoons ground cinnamon
1/2 teaspoon ground nutmeg
1/2 teaspoon ground allspice
4 ounces butter (1 stick), room temperature
1/4 cup sugar
3/4 cup brown sugar
1 egg
1/2 cup molasses
1 tablespoons corn syrup
5 bags of Sugar Babies® (1.7 oz. bags)
1/2 cup sugar for garnish

MAKE THE COOKIES

1. Preheat the oven to 375° and spray a cookie sheet with nonstick spray.

2. In a small bowl combine the flour, baking soda, salt, ginger, cloves, cinnamon, nutmeg and allspice. Set aside.

3. In a large bowl using the electric mixer, cream the butter, sugar and brown sugar. Beat in the egg, molasses and corn syrup. Mix until smooth.

4. Add the flour and spice mixture and mix thoroughly. Fold in the Sugar Babies®.

5. Using an ice cream scoop or teaspoon, scoop 1-inch balls of cookie dough onto the prepared cookie sheet, placing them 2 inches apart.

6. Place 1/2 cup of sugar in a small dish. Wet the bottom of a drinking glass. Dip the bottom of the glass into the sugar and use it to flatten cookies. Dip the glass in the sugar after flattening each cookie. Cookies should be about 1/2-inch thick.

7. Bake for 10 to 12 minutes. Cool 5 minutes before removing from cookie sheet. Makes 24 cookies.

Double Chocolate Cookies with Hershey's® Hugs®

∽ A great blend of white and dark chocolate. ∽

DIFFICULTY: 🌢🌢
EQUIPMENT: cookie sheet, double boiler, electric mixer, drinking glass

FOR THE COOKIES

24 Hershey's® Hugs®
12 ounces semi-sweet chocolate chips
4 ounces butter (1 stick), room temperature
1 cup sugar
2 eggs
1 teaspoon vanilla
1 1/2 cups flour
1/4 cup unsweetened cocoa
1 1/2 teaspoons baking powder

MAKE THE COOKIES

1. Preheat the oven to 375° and spray a cookie sheet with nonstick spray. Unwrap the Hershey's® Hugs® and set aside.

2. Melt the chocolate chips in a double boiler over medium heat and stir until smooth. Separate the double boiler and let the chocolate cool for 5 minutes.

3. In a large bowl using the electric mixer, cream the butter, sugar, eggs and vanilla. Add the flour, cocoa, baking powder and melted chocolate and mix well.

4. Shape the dough into 1-inch balls and place on prepared cookie sheet, spacing them 2 inches apart. Slightly flatten each ball of dough with the bottom of a drinking glass. If the dough sticks to the glass, clean and wet the bottom before proceeding.

5. Bake for 9 to 10 minutes.

6. Press a Hershey's® Hug® into the center of each cookie as soon they come out of the oven.

7. Transfer to a rack and cool for 1 hour. (Take care not to touch the Hershey's® Hugs® until they have completely set.) Makes about 24 cookies.

HERSHEY'S® HUGS®

The Hershey's® Hug®, introduced in 1993, is a miniature milk chocolate Kiss® enrobed or "hugged" by white chocolate and striped with ribbons of milk chocolate. Just as human hugs and kisses are executed differently, so are the methods for making Hershey's® Hugs® and Kisses®. Kisses® squirt from narrow steel pipes onto conveyor belts and Hugs® are formed in molds.

Almond Biscotti with Hershey's® Bites™

∾ A satisfying, crunchy, low-fat biscotti. ∾

DIFFICULTY: ♦♦
EQUIPMENT: cookie sheet, whisk, flour for shaping dough, serrated knife

FOR THE BISCOTTI

2 cups all-purpose flour
1 cup sugar
1 teaspoon baking powder
1/2 teaspoon baking soda
1/4 teaspoon salt
2 large eggs
2 large egg whites
1 teaspoon vanilla
1/2 teaspoon almond extract
1 1/3 cups Hershey's® Milk Chocolate with Almonds Bites™

MAKE THE BISCOTTI

1. Preheat the oven to 325° and spray a cookie sheet with nonstick spray.

2. In a large bowl, combine the flour, sugar, baking powder, baking soda and salt. Set aside.

1. In a small bowl, whisk together eggs, egg whites, vanilla and almond extract. Add the egg mixture to the dry ingredients and blend well. Fold in the Hershey's® Bites™.

4. Scoop the dough onto a floured surface and divide it in half. With well-floured hands, shape each half of dough into a 4 x 8-inch rectangle. Roll the wide side of each rectangle into a log.

5. Gently transfer the logs to the prepared cookie sheet.

6. Bake for 25 minutes, or until firm to touch.

7. Transfer the logs to a rack and cool for 15 minutes. Reduce the oven heat to 300°.

8. Using a serrated knife, cut the logs at a slight diagonal into 1/2-inch thick slices. Stand the slices upright on the baking sheet and bake for 35 to 40 minutes, or until lightly browned.

9. Cool completely or overnight before serving. Makes about 24 biscotti.

Biscotti will keep in an airtight container up to a month. It also freezes well.

HERSHEY'S® BITES™

Hershey's® Bites™ debuted in 1999. Hershey's currently offers several kinds of these round, bite-sized morsels taken from some of their most popular candy bars, including Reese's® Peanut Butter Cups, Hershey's® Milk Chocolate with Almonds, Almond Joy®, Cookies 'n' Crème® and York® Peppermint Patties.

Pay Day® Peanut Butter Cookies

⁓ Chewy peanut cluster in a classic peanut butter cookie. ⁓

DIFFICULTY: 🌑🌒

EQUIPMENT: cookie sheet, electric mixer, drinking glass

FOR THE COOKIES

5 Pay Day® Bars
2¹/₂ cups flour
¹/₂ teaspoon baking soda
¹/₂ teaspoon baking powder
¹/₄ teaspoon salt
8 ounces butter (2 sticks), room temperature
1 cup creamy peanut butter
¹/₂ cup sugar
¹/₂ cup brown sugar
2 eggs
¹/₂ teaspoon vanilla

MAKE THE COOKIES

1. Preheat the oven to 375° and spray a cookie sheet with nonstick spray.

2. Coarsely chop the candy bars and set aside.

3. In a medium bowl, combine the flour, baking soda, baking powder and salt. Set aside.

4. In a large bowl using electric mixer, cream the butter, peanut butter, sugar and brown sugar. Beat in the eggs and vanilla. Add the flour mixture and mix until thoroughly combined. Fold in the chopped candy bars.

5. Roll tablespoon-sized balls of dough between palms and place on prepared cookie sheet, 2 inches apart.

6. Flatten dough, making it ¹/₂-inch thick, with the wet bottom of a drinking glass.

7. With a fork, create a crosshatch pattern on top of each flattened cookie.

8. Bake for 9 to 12 minutes or until lightly browned. Makes 24 cookies.

PAY DAY®

Frank Martoccio was in the macaroni business in Minneapolis. According to Hershey's archives, he once had need for an electric motor. He asked local manufacturers if they had a used one they might be willing to sell. The Pratt and Langhoft Candy Company had such a motor, so Mr. Martoccio bought it. He also bought the company while he was at it. Renamed Hollywood Brands in 1933, the company produced such well-known candy bars as Zero® in 1920, Milkshake® in 1929 and Pay Day® in 1932.

Baby Ruth® Cream Cheese Brownies

∾ Cream cheese brownies—only better. ∾

DIFFICULTY: 🌢
EQUIPMENT: 13 x 9-inch pan, electric mixer

FOR THE BROWNIES

1 box brownie mix (19.8 oz.)

FOR THE CREAM CHEESE SWIRL

4 Baby Ruth Bars® (2.1 oz. bars)
8 ounces cream cheese, room temperature
1 egg
½ cup sugar
½ teaspoon vanilla

MAKE THE BROWNIES

1. Preheat the oven to 350° and spray a 13 x 9-inch pan with nonstick spray.
2. Chop the candy bars into ¼-inch chunks.

3. Prepare the brownie mix as directed on the package but do not bake.

FOR THE CREAM CHEESE SWIRL

1. In a mixing bowl, cream the softened cream cheese, egg, sugar and vanilla on high until well blended. Fold in the chopped candy bars.
2. Spread the brownie batter in the bottom of the prepared pan. Spoon the cream cheese mixture on top of the brownie batter and, with a knife or spatula, swirl the cream cheese and brownie batter together for a marble effect.
3. Bake for 35 to 40 minutes or until a toothpick inserted in the center comes out clean. Cool before cutting. Makes 18 to 24 brownies.

BABY RUTH®

Otto Schnering, founder of the Curtis Candy Company, became the father of the Baby Ruth® Bar in 1920. But legend says the father of the *real* baby Ruth was President Grover Cleveland. His daughter Ruth, born in 1891, was the first baby to be born to a president in office. She was the darling of the American public. Baby Ruth, who only lived to be 12, was immortalized when Mr. Schnering named his candy bar after her. But today most Americans think the candy bar was named for the record-hitting baseball player.

Cream Cheese Lemon Bars with Kit Kat® Crust

∽ A refreshing combination. ∽

DIFFICULTY: ▲▲

EQUIPMENT: food processor fitted with a metal blade, 8 x 8-inch square baking pan, electric mixer

FOR THE CRUST

5 Kit Kat® Bars (1.5 oz. bars)

FOR THE FILLING

8 ounces cream cheese, room temperature
2 cups powdered sugar, sifted
1 egg
2 tablespoons lemon juice
1 teaspoon lemon extract
1¹/₂ teaspoons lemon zest

FOR THE TOPPING

¹/₃ cup flour
¹/₃ cup sugar
¹/₂ teaspoon additional lemon extract
2 tablespoons butter, softened

MAKE THE CRUST

1. Preheat the oven to 400°. Spray an 8 x 8-inch pan with non-stick spray and place parchment paper in bottom of pan.
2. In the food processor, finely chop the Kit Kat® Bars and spread evenly in the pan. Bake for 5 minutes. Set aside.

MAKE THE FILLING

1. In a large bowl with electric mixer, blend the cream cheese on high. Add the powdered sugar and egg and beat until smooth, scraping down the sides of the bowl.
2. Add lemon juice, lemon extract and lemon zest, and mix well.
3. Pour filling evenly over Kit Kat® crust.

MAKE THE TOPPING

1. In a medium bowl, combine the flour, sugar, lemon extract and softened butter, and blend with a fork until crumbly.
2. Sprinkle topping evenly over lemon bar filling.
3. Bake for 18 to 20 minutes, or until topping is lightly browned. Makes 16 to 20 lemon bars.

KIT KAT®

According to journalist Joël Glenn Brenner, when Hershey's and British candy maker Rowntree decided to introduce Kit Kat® to the American market in 1973, Hershey's wanted to coat the cookies in Hershey's® chocolate because that was what they thought Americans would like. Rowntree said *No way*. So Kit Kat® was introduced to Americans with the same chocolate formula used in England. It was an immediate hit — and Hershey's learned something valuable about American tastes.

Chocolate-Covered Pretzels with Heath® Bar Sprinkles

∼ *Sweet, salty—and habit-forming.* ∼

DIFFICULTY: 🝔

EQUIPMENT: cookie sheet, wax or parchment paper, food processor fitted with a metal blade, double boiler

FOR THE CHOCOLATE PRETZELS

3 Heath® Bars (1.4 oz. bars)
1 cup milk chocolate chips
24 miniature pretzels (2-inch pretzels)

MAKE THE CHOCOLATE PRETZELS

1. Line a cookie sheet with wax or parchment paper.

2. In the food processor, finely chop the Heath® Bars. Transfer to a shallow, medium-sized bowl.

3. Melt the milk chocolate chips in a double boiler over medium heat. As soon as the chocolate has melted, remove from the heat.

4. Working quickly, dip each pretzel in the melted chocolate one at a time, turning to coat entire pretzel.

5. Roll each chocolate-coated pretzel in chopped Heath® Bars and place on the prepared cookie sheet.

6. Let the chocolate coating set 30 minutes before serving. Store in a cool, airtight container. Makes 24 chocolate-covered pretzels.

HEATH® ENGLISH TOFFEE BARS

L. S. Heath and his two sons first made the Heath® Bar in 1928 in Robinson, Illinois. According to candy historian Ray Broekel, Americans often called these "H and H" bars in the early days. The original wrapper featured two large capital H's on either side of the lower-cased word "eat": a play on the name Heath—or *Eat "H and H."*

THE HISTORY OF THE PRETZEL

According to pretzel lore, in 610 A.D. a monk rolled scraps of leftover bread dough into long, slender pieces and twisted them to look like arms folded over a chest in prayer. He called his prayer knots *pretiola*, which means "little reward" in Latin. Children were often given a pretiola when they learned their prayers. Pretzels were twisted by hand until machines were developed in 1933 to automate the process.

Roll out the Candy!

~ Pies and Tarts ~

Hershey's® Cookies 'n' Mint Mousse Pie

∾ Wicked good. ∾

DIFFICULTY: 🌢🌢🌢

EQUIPMENT: food processor fitted with a metal blade, 9-inch pie pan, drinking glass (as needed), double boiler, electric mixer

FOR THE CRUST

14 OREO® Chocolate Sandwich Cookies
4 tablespoons butter, melted

FOR THE FILLING

41 Hershey's® Cookies 'n' Mint Nuggets™
  (13 oz. bag), reserve 3 for garnish
6 ounces butter (1½ sticks)
6 egg whites (Note: Many grocery stores carry
  pasteurized egg whites by the pint.)
2 tablespoons sugar

FOR THE WHIPPED CREAM TOPPING

2 cups whipped cream
¼ cup unsweetened cocoa
¼ cup powdered sugar, sifted

MAKE THE CRUST

1. Preheat the oven to 375°.

2. In the food processor, finely crush the OREO® cookies. Add melted butter to the crumb mixture and continue processing until well blended.

3. Transfer the mixture to a 9-inch pie pan and press evenly over the bottom and up the sides of the pan.

4. Bake for 10 minutes. The crust may rise slightly during baking. Use the flat bottom of a drinking glass to gently press down the crust. Cool completely before filling.

MAKE THE FILLING

1. In a double boiler, over medium-low heat, melt the Hershey's® Nuggets™ and butter together, stirring until chocolate is melted. (There will be cookie crumbs in the chocolate.) Separate the double boiler and cool for 30 minutes.

2. In a separate bowl, using an electric mixer, beat the egg whites until foamy. Gradually add sugar and beat until stiff peaks form.

3. Fold about 2 cups of the egg whites into the chocolate mixture. Now pour the chocolate mixture back into the remaining egg whites and fold gently until uniform in color.

4. Pour into cooled piecrust and cover with plastic wrap. Refrigerate for 1 hour or up to 2 days before serving.

MAKE THE WHIPPED CREAM TOPPING

NOTE: Prepare the topping just before serving the pie.

1. Combine the cream, cocoa and powdered sugar in a large bowl and beat until mixture doubles in size and forms stiff peaks. Mound the topping evenly over filling.

2. Coarsely chop reserved 3 Hershey's® Cookies 'n' Mint Nuggets™ and sprinkle evenly over top of whipped cream. Serves 8 to 10.

HERSHEY'S® COOKIES 'N' MINT NUGGETS™

Hershey's® Cookies 'n' Mint Nuggets™ debuted in 1994, following the success of Hershey's® Cookies 'n' Mint™ bar in 1992.

Chocolate Peppermint Pillow Pie

∞ *One of Ric's childhood favorites.* ∞

For the very best results, this pie should be made three days prior to serving and can be made as many as six days ahead. The whipped cream softens the cookie crumbs, mints and marshmallows, making for an amazing creamy, crunchy peppermint treat.

DIFFICULTY: ◣◢
EQUIPMENT: food processor fitted with a metal blade, 13 x 9-inch pan, electric mixer

For the Bottom Layer

1 package OREO® Chocolate Sandwich Cookies (1 pound package)

For the Top Layer

1½ pints whipping cream
¾ cup powdered sugar, sifted
½ teaspoon vanilla
2 cups mini-marshmallows
1 cup Brach's® Dessert Mints (pastel pillow mints)

Make the Bottom Layer

1. In the food processor, finely chop the OREO® cookies.
2. Pour half the crumbs into bottom of a 13 x 9-inch pan and spread evenly. Do not pack down the cookie crumbs. Set the rest of the crumbs aside.

Make the Top Layer

1. In a large mixing bowl, combine the cream, powdered sugar and vanilla. Beat until stiff peaks form. Spoon the whipped cream on top of the cookie crumbs and spread gently but evenly.
2. Distribute the mini-marshmallows and mints evenly over top of the whipped cream.
3. Sprinkle the remaining cookie crumbs on top of the pie.
4. Cover tightly with plastic wrap and refrigerate 3 days before serving. Serves 18.

BRACH'S® DESSERT MINTS

Emil J. Brach began his career in 1881 as a candy salesman for a caramel company. In 1904, he opened his own candy shop called Brach's Palace of Sweets. The caramels he made in the back of his store earned him a sweet reputation in and around the Chicago area.

As Brach's business grew, his sons joined the company, and they began manufacturing other confections such as jellybeans, chocolate bars and jawbreakers. Today, Brach's sells packaged American favorites, including dessert mints, peppermints, Milkmaid® Caramels, circus peanuts, candy corn and jelly beans.

Dots® Tartlets

∾ Dazzling and tasty for Dots® fans. ∾

DIFFICULTY: ♦♦♦

EQUIPMENT: Four 4-inch fluted tart pans, electric mixer, rolling pin, flour for rolling, sharp knife, fork, whisk

FOR THE CRUST

8 ounces butter (2 sticks), room temperature
1/2 cup sugar
2 eggs
1 teaspoon vanilla
1/4 teaspoon salt
2 1/2 cups all-purpose flour
1/2 cup white chocolate chips

FOR THE PASTRY CREAM

1/4 cup corn starch
1/4 cup sugar
1 egg
2 egg yolks
2 cups milk
1/4 cup additional sugar
2 tablespoons butter
1 teaspoon vanilla

(You may substitute 1 small box of instant vanilla pudding for the pastry cream.

Prepare pudding according to directions on package. Cool pudding and cover with plastic wrap until ready to assemble tarts.)

FOR THE TOPPING

2 large boxes of Dots® (7 oz. each)

MAKE THE CRUST

1. In a large bowl using electric mixer, cream the butter and sugar on medium. Beat in the eggs, vanilla and salt. Add flour and mix on low until dough forms.

2. Using hands, shape dough into a 4-inch round disk. Wrap the dough in plastic wrap and refrigerate for at least an hour.

3. Preheat the oven to 375°.

4. Remove dough from the refrigerator and divide it into 4 equal parts. Working dough between hands to soften, shape each piece of dough into a ball and flatten it into a circle. On a floured surface, roll each circle to 1/4-inch thick round.

5. Place each round in a tart pan, gently pressing dough into the fluted sides. Using a sharp knife, trim excess dough

continued on next page

evenly with the top of each tart pan. Using the tines of a fork, poke a few holes in the bottom of each crust to prevent bubbles from forming.

6. Bake for 10 to 15 minutes or until crust is light golden brown.

7. As soon as crusts come out of the oven, sprinkle white chocolate chips over the bottom of each tart shell. Let the chips soften for 5 minutes.

8. Spread melted white chocolate evenly over crusts. Allow the crusts to cool completely before assembling.

MAKE THE PASTRY CREAM

1. In a medium bowl using electric mixer, blend together the cornstarch, ¼ cup sugar, egg and egg yolks.

2. In a heavy saucepan, bring the milk and additional ¼ cup sugar to a boil. Remove pan from heat and immediately whisk cornstarch mixture into hot milk mixture. Whisk vigorously to avoid eggs cooking on contact with hot milk.

3. Return saucepan to medium-low heat and continue whisking until mixture thickens and begins to boil. Remove saucepan from heat and stir in butter and vanilla.

4. Cover with plastic wrap so wrap touches entire surface of the pastry cream. Cool completely. (Will keep covered in the refrigerator for up to one week.)

ASSEMBLE THE TARTLETS

1. Place a generous spoonful of pastry cream or vanilla pudding into each cooled tart shell and spread evenly.

2. Arrange the Dots® on top of the pastry cream in concentric circles, beginning in the center and working out to the rim. To ensure the outer circle of Dots® will fit snugly, trim the sides of the Dots® that will touch the edge of the crust.

3. Lightly brush the Dots® with water just before serving for a glistening look. Serves 4.

DOTS®

In the 1890's, Ernest Von Au and Joseph Maison created a line of licorice gumdrops called Black Rose. When the candy wrappers came off the presses, however, the name read Black Crows; the printer had misunderstood their request. Rather than reprint the wrappers, the candy makers kept the name Black Crows® for their licorice drops. The Mason Company soon followed with fruit-flavored gumdrops called Dots®, as well as Spice Berries®, Cherry Dots® and most recently Tropical Dots®.

Ghirardelli® White Chocolate and Lemon Mousse Pie

∽ *A wonderfully light summer dessert.* ∽

DIFFICULTY: ▲▲▲

EQUIPMENT: food processor fitted with a metal blade, 9-inch pie pan, double boiler, electric mixer

FOR THE CRUST

40 Nilla® Wafers Cookies
3 tablespoons butter, melted

FOR THE MOUSSE

2 teaspoons lemon zest (zest of 2 lemons), grated or finely chopped
4 teaspoons lemon juice (juice of same 2 lemons)
8 ounces Ghirardelli® Classic White Confection (or two 4 oz. bars)
2 1/2 cups whipping cream
2 teaspoons unflavored gelatin
2 tablespoons water
1 1/2 teaspoons lemon extract

MAKE THE CRUST

1. Preheat the oven to 375°.
2. In the food processor, finely crush the Nilla® Wafers.
3. Add the melted butter to the cookie crumbs and continue processing until well blended.
4. Transfer the mixture to a 9-inch pie pan and press crust evenly over the bottom and up the sides of the pan.
5. Bake for 6 to 8 minutes, or until lightly browned. Cool completely before filling.

MAKE THE MOUSSE

1. Place the lemon zest in a small dish and add two teaspoons of lemon juice.
2. Finely chop the white chocolate and place in a medium bowl. Set aside.
3. Boil 1/2 cup of whipping cream in the microwave, about 60 seconds on high. Pour the hot cream over the white chocolate and stir until smooth. Set aside.

continued on next page

4. Mix the gelatin and water in a small bowl and let stand for 2 minutes. Microwave on high for 40 seconds and stir until dissolved.

5. Add the dissolved gelatin, lemon zest and lemon juice to the white chocolate mixture and stir until smooth. Set aside.

6. In a large bowl, whip the remaining 2 cups of cream and the lemon extract until stiff peaks form.

7. Add one-half of the whipped cream to the white chocolate mixture and fold together.

8. Gently fold entire white chocolate mixture into the remaining whipped cream.

9. Pour the mousse into the cooled crust.

10. Cover with plastic and refrigerate for 1 hour or up to 2 days before serving. Serves 10.

Garnish with long curls of lemon zest if desired.

GHIRARDELLI® CHOCOLATE

Italian-born Domingo Ghirardelli had one thing on his mind when he boarded a ship bound for California in 1849: gold. Ghirardelli did strike it rich, but his mother lode was chocolate. It took 40 years of selling groceries and provisions, operating soda fountains and manufacturing syrups, spices, teas, wines, liquors, coffee and, of course, chocolate to establish what is still a booming chocolate business in San Francisco.

According to company history, Ghirardelli discovered the "broma process," a way of extracting cocoa butter from chocolate to make cocoa powder. The company still uses the same process today as they did in the 1860's to create some of America's best-loved specialty chocolate.

Peanut Butterfinger® Pie

∽ Ric highly recommends this one. ∽

DIFFICULTY: ♦♦♦

EQUIPMENT: food processor fitted with a metal blade, 9-inch pie pan, drinking glass (as needed), electric mixer, whisk

FOR THE CRUST

14 OREO® Chocolate Sandwich Cookies
4 tablespoons butter, melted

FOR THE FILLING

7 Butterfinger® Bars (2.1 oz. bars), 1 coarsely chopped for garnish
1/2 cup sugar
2 tablespoons cornstarch
2 cups milk
2 egg yolks
1/2 cup creamy peanut butter
1/2 cup chocolate chips
1 1/2 cups whipping cream

FOR THE TOPPING

2 cups whipping cream

MAKE THE CRUST

1. Preheat the oven to 375°.

2. In the food processor, finely crush the OREO® cookies. Add the melted butter to the cookie crumbs and continue processing until well blended.

3. Transfer the mixture to a 9-inch pie pan and press evenly over the bottom and up the sides of the pan.

4. Bake for 8 minutes. The crust may rise slightly during baking. Use the flat bottom of a drinking glass to gently press down the crust. Cool completely before filling.

MAKE THE FILLING

1. In the food processor, finely chop 6 candy bars and divide into two 1/2-cup portions and one 1-cup portion and set aside.

2. In a medium saucepan combine the sugar, cornstarch, milk and egg yolks. Place the saucepan on medium-high heat, stirring constantly until mixture thickens and begins to boil. Remove from heat.

continued on next page

3. Add peanut butter and whisk until smooth.

4. Set aside 1 cup of peanut butter mixture in a medium mixing bowl. Cover with plastic wrap.

5. Add the chocolate chips and $1/2$ cup of finely chopped candy bars to remaining mixture in the saucepan. Stir until chips are melted.

6. Pour this mixture into the cooled crust.

7. Cover with plastic wrap so the wrap lies flat against the entire surface of the chocolate layer, and refrigerate.

MAKE THE PEANUT BUTTER LAYER

1. Whip $1^1/2$ cups cream until stiff peaks form. Fold in reserved cooled peanut butter mixture and $1/2$ cup of finely chopped candy bars.

2. Remove pie from refrigerator and remove plastic. Mound peanut butter mixture evenly over chocolate layer and spread to the edges.

MAKE THE TOPPING

1. In a medium bowl, whip 2 cups of cream until stiff peaks form.

2. Fold in 1 cup of finely chopped candy bars.

3. Spoon the whipped cream evenly over filling.

4. Sprinkle the coarsely chopped candy bar on top of the pie.

5. Cover loosely and refrigerate until ready to serve. Serves 10.

BUTTERFINGER®

How would you feel if your favorite candy bar floated into your backyard by parachute? This really happened in towns across America in the 1920's. Long before Bart Simpson pledged his allegiance to the Butterfinger® Bar, Mr. Otto Schnering hired pilots to shower bundles of Butterfinger® and Baby Ruth® Bars on selected American cities. Today, those wafer-thin layers of toffee still crumble into peanut butter shards— not on the back patio, but when when you bite into a Butterfinger.®

Hershey's® Classic Caramels Apple Tart

~ Caramel apples for grown-ups. ~

DIFFICULTY: ▲▲▲

EQUIPMENT: One 8-inch fluted tart pan or 9-inch pie pan; flour for rolling, rolling pin, electric mixer

FOR THE CRUST

3 tablespoons butter, room temperature
3 tablespoons sugar
1 egg
¼ teaspoon vanilla
1½ cups all-purpose flour
pinch of salt
¼ cup chocolate chips

FOR THE FILLING

14 Hershey's® Classic Caramels, unwrapped
2 teaspoons milk
2 Granny Smith apples
juice of 1 lemon

MAKE THE CRUST

1. Using an electric mixer, cream the butter and sugar on high until light pale and fluffy.

2. Add in the eggs and vanilla and beat until fully incorporated.

3. Mix in the flour and salt on low until dough forms.

4. Shape dough into a 4-inch round disk and wrap in plastic. Refrigerate for at least an hour.

5. Preheat the oven to 375°.

6. Remove the dough from the refrigerator and divide it into 2 pieces. Using hands, work dough to soften.

7. Combine the 2 pieces of softened dough into one 4-inch round disk. Place the dough on a floured surface and roll it out into a 10-inch circle, ⅛-inch thick. (For a 9-inch pie pan, make an 11-inch circle.)

8. Place the rolled dough in the tart pan and drape excess over edges. Starting with the middle of the crust, gently pat

the dough down to remove any air pockets and gently push dough down into the flutes of the pan.

9. Using a knife, trim the excess dough evenly with the top of the tart pan. Using the tines of a fork, poke holes in the bottom of the crust to prevent bubbles from forming.

10. Bake 15 minutes or until crust is lightly golden brown.

11. As soon as the crust comes out of the oven, pour the chocolate chips evenly over the bottom of the tart shell. Let the chips soften for about 5 minutes. Spread evenly over the bottom of the crust. (The chocolate will later protect the crust from the juice of the sliced apples.) Allow the crust to cool completely. Can be tightly wrapped and refrigerated at this point for up to a week or frozen up to a month.

MAKE THE FILLING

1. Melt the caramels in a medium saucepan over medium-low heat, stirring until smooth.

2. While the caramels are melting, core and slice the apples into $1/8$-inch slices. Sprinkle with lemon juice to preserve color and then lightly press the apple slices on a paper towel to remove excess juice.

3. Arrange the apples in the bottom of the crust in a pinwheel, slightly overlapping each slice.

4. Pour melted caramel evenly over apples. Allow the caramel to cool for 10 minutes before serving. Serves 8.

NOTE: For best appearance, assemble the tart no more than a few hours before serving, as the juice of the apples will begin to run.

HERSHEY'S® CLASSIC CARAMELS

The candy that put Milton Hershey on the map was actually caramel. In 1886 Hershey founded the Lancaster Caramel Company. According to Hershey's company history, he saw an exhibit in Chicago that included chocolate-making machinery from Germany. Intrigued, he bought the machinery and began to top his caramels with chocolate. In 1900 Hershey sold his caramel business to pursue chocolate full-time. In a return to their founder's roots, Hershey's began to manufacture caramels in the 1990's after more than a 100-year hiatus.

Whoppers® Chocolate Pie

⌇ A malted milk ball lover's fantasy. ⌇

DIFFICULTY: 🌶🌶
EQUIPMENT: 9-inch pie pan, food processor fitted with a metal blade, drinking glass (as needed), double boiler, electric mixer

For the Crust

14 OREO® Chocolate Sandwich Cookies
4 tablespoons butter, melted

For the Filling

1 square (1 oz.) unsweetened baking chocolate
1 cup Whoppers®
4 ounces butter (1 stick), room temperature
³/₄ cup sugar
2 eggs (okay to use egg substitute)

For the Topping

2 cups whipping cream
¹/₂ cup powdered sugar, sifted
¹/₂ teaspoon vanilla
¹/₂ cup additional Whoppers®, coarsely chopped
10 Whoppers® whole, for garnish

Make the Crust

1. Preheat the oven to 375°.

2. In the food processor, finely chop the OREO® cookies.

3. Add melted butter to the cookie crumbs and continue processing until well blended.

4. Transfer the mixture to a 9-inch pie pan and press evenly over the bottom and up the sides of the pan.

5. Bake for 10 minutes. Mixture may rise slightly during baking. Use the flat bottom of a drinking glass to gently press down the crust. Cool completely before filling.

Make the Filling

1. In a double boiler over medium heat, warm the unsweetened chocolate until just melted. Stir until smooth. Remove from heat and separate the double boiler. Cool the chocolate for 5 minutes.

2. Coarsely chop 1 cup Whoppers® into ¹/₈-inch pieces and set aside.

3. In a large mixing bowl, cream the butter

and sugar for 2 minutes with mixer on high. Add the melted chocolate and 1 egg. Mix for 1 minute on medium-high. Add the second egg and mix for 1 more minute. Fold in the coarsely chopped Whoppers®.

4. Transfer the filling into the cooled crust and spread evenly over the bottom.

5. Cover in plastic wrap and refrigerate.

MAKE THE TOPPING

1. In a large mixing bowl, combine the cream, powdered sugar and vanilla. Beat until stiff peaks form.

2. Fold in ½ cup coarsely chopped Whoppers®.

3. Using a wooden spoon, spread the whipped cream evenly over filling.

4. Garnish decoratively with whole Whoppers®. Serves 8 to 10.

WHOPPERS®

When Whoppers® malted milk balls debuted in 1939, they were called Giants®. In those days, they sold 2 for a penny. After cellophane was introduced in the 1940's, Whoppers® were packaged 5 for a penny and were known as "fivesomes." The Whopper® milk carton was also introduced in the 1940's. Whopper® Easter Eggs and Robin's Eggs hatched in the late 1940's and 1950's. Mint Whoppers® and Peanut Butter Whoppers® made a brief appearance in the 1970's.

3 Musketeers® Meringue Pie

~ Imagine 3 Musketeers® with a cookie crust and meringue topping. ~

DIFFICULTY: ▲▲▲

EQUIPMENT: food processor fitted with a metal blade, 9-inch pie pan, electric mixer

FOR THE CRUST

40 Nilla® Wafers cookies
3 tablespoons butter, melted

FOR THE FILLING

3 3 Musketeers® Bars (2.13 oz. bars)
1/2 cup sugar
2 tablespoons cornstarch
1 1/2 cups milk
2 egg yolks

FOR THE MERINGUE

3 egg whites
1/4 teaspoon cream of tartar
1/4 cup sugar

MAKE THE CRUST

1. Preheat the oven to 400°.

2. In the food processor, finely crush the Nilla® Wafer cookies.

3. Add the melted butter to the cookie crumbs and continue processing until blended.

4. Transfer the mixture to a 9-inch pie pan and press evenly over the bottom and up the sides of the pan. Bake for 6 to 8 minutes, or until lightly browned. Cool completely before filling.

MAKE THE FILLING

1. Slice the candy bars into 1/4-inch slices and set aside.

2. In a medium saucepan, combine sugar, cornstarch, milk and egg yolks. Stir well to blend.

3. Place the saucepan over medium-high heat, stirring constantly until the mixture thickens and begins to boil. Remove from heat.

continued on next page

4. Add the sliced 3 Musketeers® Bars and stir until candy melts and mixture is smooth.

5. Pour mixture into the prepared crust.

MAKE THE MERINGUE

1. Preheat oven to 400°.

2. In a clean, dry mixing bowl, beat egg whites and cream of tartar until foamy.

3. Gradually add the sugar, continuing to beat until the egg whites form stiff peaks.

4. Gently spread the egg whites over the pie filling, completely covering top of pie to edges of the crust.

5. Bake for 8 to 10 minutes, or until the peaks are golden.

6. Remove from oven and cool completely before serving. Store refrigerated. Serves 8 to 10.

3 MUSKETEERS®

The original 3 Musketeers®, introduced in 1932, included three separate pieces of candy in one wrapper. Each "mini musketeer" in the package had different flavored nougat—chocolate, vanilla or strawberry—all sheathed in milk chocolate. Strawberries proved to be an expensive ingredient during the Depression years, so Frank Mars chose to use the chocolate nougat filling when he decided to make the one big bar we know today.

Candy Bars
Take the Cake!
Layer Cakes, Cheesecake and Soufflés

Milky Way® Chocolate Cake with Caramel Buttercream Frosting

∞ *This was a big hit at our Wednesday Night Dessert Club.* ∞

DIFFICULTY: 🔺🔺🔺
EQUIPMENT: Two 9-inch round cake pans, parchment paper (optional), electric mixer, wire rack

FOR THE CAKE

3 Milky Way® Bars (2.05 oz. bars)
1 3/4 cups milk, plus 2 tablespoons
3/4 cup unsweetened cocoa
2 cups flour
1 tablespoon baking powder
1/2 teaspoon baking soda
1/4 teaspoon salt
4 ounces butter (1 stick), room temperature
1 cup sugar
1/2 cup brown sugar
1/2 teaspoon vanilla
2 eggs

FOR THE FROSTING

50 caramels (we recommend Hershey's® Classic Caramels)

1/2 cup milk
8 ounces butter (2 sticks), room temperature
5 cups powdered sugar, sifted
1/2 teaspoon vanilla

MAKE THE CAKE

1. In a heavy saucepan over medium-low heat, melt the candy bars with 2 tablespoons milk. Stir until smooth. Remove from heat and cool for 10 minutes.

2. Preheat the oven to 350° and lightly butter and flour two 9-inch round cake pans. (We also recommend lining cake pans with parchment paper.)

3. In a medium bowl combine the cocoa, flour, baking powder, baking soda and salt. Set aside.

4. In a large bowl, cream together the butter, sugar, brown sugar and vanilla on high until well blended.

5. Add the eggs one at a time and beat for 30 seconds on high, scraping down the sides of the bowl after each addition.

6. Add the melted Milky Way® mixture and mix for 30 seconds on high.

7. Add one-half of the flour mixture and one-half the remaining milk to the butter mixture and mix well, scraping down the sides of the bowl.

8. Add the remaining flour mixture and milk. Mix until thoroughly incorporated.

9. Pour the batter into the prepared cake pans.

10. Bake for 28 to 30 minutes or until a toothpick inserted in the middle of the cake comes out clean.

11. Cool the cakes in the pans for 10 minutes. Invert the cakes onto a rack and cool completely before frosting.

MAKE THE FROSTING

1. In a medium saucepan over medium-low heat, melt the caramels, stirring often. Remove from heat and stir in milk until smooth. Set aside and cool to room temperature.

2. In a medium mixing bowl, cream together butter, powdered sugar and vanilla for 3 minutes on high.

3. Add the cooled caramel mixture and mix on high for 2 minutes.

FROST THE CAKE

1. Place one cake layer on a serving plate and spread one-third of frosting over the top.

2. Place the second cake layer on top. Spread the remaining frosting over the top and sides of the cake. Serves 10 to 12.

MILKY WAY®

Frank C. Mars introduced the Milky Way® Bar in 1923. According to candy journalist Joël Glenn Brenner, the idea originated in an offhand remark made by Mars's son, Forrest. Sipping a chocolate malt, Forrest suggested that his father put something like his malt into a candy bar. So Frank did and the American public loved it. No one had ever had a candy bar with a fluffy nougat center before. Ordinary bars of chocolate seemed flat in size and value next to this new puffed-up contender.

Raisinets® Carrot Cake

∽ *A 4-star carrot cake.* ∽

DIFFICULTY: ◢◣◢

EQUIPMENT: Two 9-inch round cake pans, parchment paper (optional), food processor fitted with a grating blade, electric mixer, wire rack

FOR THE CAKE

1 2/3 cup canola oil
1 cup sugar
1 cup brown sugar
4 eggs
3 cups flour
2 teaspoons baking powder
1 1/2 teaspoons baking soda
1/2 teaspoon salt
3 teaspoons ground cinnamon
1 1/2 cups grated carrots
1/4 cup pineapple, drained and pressed
5 bags Raisinets® (1.5 oz. bags)

FOR THE FROSTING

12 ounces cream cheese, room temperature
6 cups powdered sugar, sifted
2 ounces butter (1/2 stick), room temperature
1 teaspoon vanilla

MAKE THE CAKE

1. Preheat the oven to 350° and lightly butter and flour two 9-inch round cake pans. (We also recommend lining cake pans with parchment paper.)

2. In a large bowl, mix the canola oil, sugar, brown sugar and eggs for 2 minutes on high.

3. Add the flour, baking powder, baking soda, salt and cinnamon to egg mixture and mix on medium speed until well blended.

4. Fold in the grated carrots, drained pineapple and Raisinets®.

5. Pour the batter evenly into the prepared cake pans.

6. Bake for 38 to 40 minutes, or until a toothpick inserted in the center of the cake comes out clean.

7. Remove from oven and cool cakes for 15 minutes in pans. Invert cakes onto a rack and cool completely before frosting.

continued on next page

MAKE THE FROSTING

1. With an electric mixer, blend cream cheese and butter on high until smooth and fluffy.
2. Add the powdered sugar and mix on low until well blended.
3. Add the vanilla and beat on high for 1 minute.

FROST THE CAKE

1 Place one cake layer on a serving plate. Spread one-third of the frosting over the top.
2 Place second layer of cake on top. Spread the remaining frosting over the top and sides of the cake. Serves 10.

Hershey's® Kisses® Cake

If you like Hershey's® Kisses®, then kiss your other chocolate cake recipes goodbye.

DIFFICULTY: ▲▲

EQUIPMENT: Two 9-inch round cake pans, parchment paper (optional), double boiler, electric mixer, wire rack

FOR THE CAKE

40 Hershey's® Kisses®, chopped (a total of 27 oz. of Kisses® for cake and frosting)
¹/₃ cup milk
1 cup mayonnaise
2 cups sugar
4 eggs
1 teaspoon vanilla
2 cups flour
1 cup unsweetened cocoa
2 teaspoons baking soda
³/₄ cup water

FOR THE WHIPPED CREAM FROSTING

112 Hershey's® Kisses®, set aside 12 for garnish
2 tablespoons butter
10 ounces whipping cream

MAKE THE CAKE

1. Preheat the oven to 350° and lightly butter and flour two 9-inch round cake pans. (We also recommend lining cake pans with parchment paper.)

2. In a double boiler over medium heat, melt 40 Hershey's® Kisses® with milk. Stir until smooth. Separate the double boiler and allow the chocolate mixture to cool for 10 minutes.

3. In a large bowl, using an electric mixer, cream together mayonnaise, sugar, eggs and vanilla on high.

4. Mix in the flour, cocoa, baking soda and water. Blend on medium, scraping down the sides of the bowl.

5. Add the melted chocolate mixture and incorporate thoroughly.

6. Pour equal amounts of batter into the prepared cake pans and bake for 30 to 35 minutes, or until a toothpick inserted in the center of the cake comes out clean.

continued on next page

7. Cool cakes in pans for 15 minutes. Invert onto a rack and cool completely.

Make Whipped Cream Frosting

1. In a double boiler over medium heat, melt 100 Hershey's Kisses® and butter. Stir until smooth. Separate the double boiler and cool the melted chocolate mixture to room temperature.

2. In a large mixing bowl, combine the cooled chocolate mixture and half of the cream. Mix on high for 30 seconds.

3. Place bowl in the refrigerator for 30 minutes.

4. Remove from refrigerator, and add remaining cream and whip on high until stiff peaks form.

Frost the Cake

1. Place one cake layer on a serving plate. Spread one-third of frosting over top. Place the second layer on top.

2. Spread the remaining frosting over the top and sides of the cake.

3. Garnish the rim of the cake with 12 unwrapped Hershey's® Kisses®. Serves 12.

A KISS IS JUST A KISS

A real kiss makes a wonderful little suction noise when it's placed on an object of affection. When the chocolate for a Hershey's® Kiss® squirts from a slender steel pipe onto a conveyor belt, it also makes a sound like a kiss. Legend says the Hershey's® Kiss® was named after this kissing sound.

Milton Hershey began to produce chocolate Kisses® in 1907. Each Kiss® was hand-wrapped until 1921. The little white streamers bearing the light blue Hershey's® trademark were added in 1924. Today the Kiss® still retains its original size and shape. It has been said that Milton Hershey's mother, Fanny Hershey, passed away while wrapping Hershey's® Kisses® in her kitchen across the street from the factory.

Marshmallow Fudge Cake

~ This has been Alison's favorite cake since childhood. Thanks, Mom. ~

DIFFICULTY: ♦♦

EQUIPMENT: 9-inch square baking pan, parchment paper (optional), scissors

FOR THE CAKE

½ cup boiling water
2 squares unsweetened baking chocolate (1 oz. each)
2 eggs
1½ cups sugar
½ cup sour cream
½ cup canola oil
1½ cups flour
1 teaspoon baking soda

FOR THE FUDGE FROSTING

16-18 marshmallows
2½ squares unsweetened chocolate (1 oz. each)
⅓ cup butter
1¼ cup sugar
⅓ cup milk
1 teaspoon vanilla

MAKE THE CAKE

1. Preheat the oven to 350°. Lightly butter and flour a 9-inch square baking pan. (We also recommend lining cake pans with parchment paper.)

2. In a heavy saucepan over medium-high heat, bring the water to a boil. Remove from heat. Add the chocolate to the hot water and stir until smooth.

3. In a large bowl, beat the eggs and sugar on medium. Beat in the sour cream and oil.

4. Add the melted chocolate and mix thoroughly.

5. Stir in the flour and baking soda.

6. Pour the batter into the prepared cake pan and bake for 35 to 40 minutes, or until a toothpick inserted in the center of the cake comes out clean.

7. Let the cake cool for 5 minutes in pan. Invert onto a serving plate.

continued on next page

Prepare the Marshmallows

1. Fill a medium mixing bowl half full with warm water.

2. Using scissors, cut the marshmallows into thirds, so each slice is round.

3. Place the marshmallows in the warm water and soak for one minute.

4. Immediately remove marshmallows from water and cover the entire top of the cake with a layer of wet marshmallow slices.

Make the Fudge Frosting

1. In a heavy saucepan over medium-low heat, melt the chocolate and butter together and stir until smooth.

2. Stir in the sugar, milk and vanilla.

3. Increase heat to medium, stirring constantly. Bring the mixture to a rapid boil and boil for 1 minute, still stirring. Remove from the heat and let the chocolate mixture stand 2 minutes.

4. Using an electric mixer, beat the frosting 5 to 6 minutes. The frosting will be pourable, but thick enough so it will just run down the sides. (Overmixing will make the frosting too thick.)

5. Pour frosting over the marshmallows and spread it with a spatula, letting it drip down the sides. Serves 10 to 12.

THE MARSHMALLOW

The mallow plant grows in marshes. It has pink flowers and a sweet, sticky sap inside its roots. The ancient Egyptians are thought to have discovered that the sweet sap could be extracted and used in confections. Nearly 4000 years later, mallow sap was replaced with gelatin to make the production of marshmallows more efficient. But the name marshmallow stuck. Today these pillowy confections are squeezed from steel pipes instead of stems.

Special Dark® Ganache Cake
with Chocolate-Dipped Strawberries

~ Originally called Double Chocolate Suicide, this is Ric's signature dessert. ~

DIFFICULTY: ♦♦♦

EQUIPMENT: Four 9-inch round cake pans, parchment paper (optional), double boiler, electric mixer, wire rack, plastic wrap

FOR THE CAKE

2 boxes of Devil's Food Cake mix (18.25 oz. each)

FOR THE CHOCOLATE GANACHE

16 Hershey's Special Dark® Bars (1.45 oz. bars), coarsely chopped
1/4 teaspoon freeze-dried coffee
3 tablespoons butter
1 pint whipping cream

FOR THE CHOCOLATE DIPPED STRAWBERRIES

12 large ripe strawberries, rinsed, drained and dried
1/2 cup chocolate ganache (reserved from above)

MAKE THE CAKES

1. Preheat the oven to 350° and lightly butter and flour two 9-inch round cake pans. (We recommend lining cake pans with parchment paper.)

2. Bake both boxes of cake mix (for a total of 4 cake layers) as directed on box. (If only two cake pans are available, bake two layers at a time, proceeding with recipe when all four layers are baked and cooled.)

3. Cool cakes in the pans for 10 minutes. Invert onto cooling racks and cool completely.

4. Wrap each cool layer tightly in plastic wrap and refrigerate the cakes for two hours. (Cakes may be baked 2 days ahead and stored in the refrigerator.)

WHILE THE CAKE BAKES, MAKE THE GANACHE

1. In a double boiler over medium heat, melt the candy bars with freeze-dried coffee and butter. Stir often.

2. Remove from heat and separate the double boiler.

3. Pour one-third of cream on top of the

continued on next page

chocolate. With a spatula, stir until smooth.

4. Add the remaining cream, and again, stir until smooth. Set aside.

5. Reserve $1/2$ cup of ganache for dipping strawberries to garnish the cake.

FOR THE GANACHE CAKE

1. Place two clean 9-inch round cake pans on a flat surface. Center a 20-inch piece of plastic wrap over each pan and set aside.

2. Place three of the baked and cooled chocolate cakes in a large mixing bowl.

3. Using the electric mixer on low, coarsely crumble the cakes.

4. Pour $1 1/2$ cups of chocolate ganache over the crumbled cake mixture and blend for 1 minute on low until combined.

5. Divide ganache cake mixture into 2 equal parts. Place one-half in each plastic-lined cake pan.

6. Pack the mixture evenly into each pan. (Each round will be about 1-inch tall.)

7. Fold extra plastic wrap over to cover center of each cake. Wrap again completely with plastic wrap.

8. Place ganache cakes and remaining wrapped plain Devil's Food cake in freezer for 2 hours, or refrigerate overnight.

9. Cover and set aside remaining ganache.

ASSEMBLE THE CAKE

1. Reheat the ganache in a double boiler over medium-low heat, stirring occasionally until warm.

2. Remove cakes from refrigerator. Unwrap and place one of the ganache cake layers on a serving platter.

3. Pour $1/4$ cup of ganache on top of this layer. (This will act as a "glue" between layers, not frosting.)

4. Unwrap the remaining intact Devil's Food cake layer and place on top.

5. Pour another $1/4$ cup of ganache on top of this layer.

6. Unwrap the second ganache cake and place on top.

7. Pour remaining ganache over the entire surface, letting it drip down the sides.

8. Smooth the chocolate on the sides of the cake to match the satin coating on top.

FOR THE CHOCOLATE-DIPPED STRAWBERRIES

1. Reheat the reserved $1/2$ cup of ganache in a double boiler over medium-low heat, stirring occasionally until warm.

2. Dip each strawberry in chocolate ganache and place decoratively around the edge or on top of the cake. Serves 16 to 18.

HERSHEY'S® SPECIAL DARK®

Hershey's dark chocolate recipe has been modified four times in the past 63 years to suit the changing tastes of America's dark chocolate palate. The first recipe debuted in 1937 and was called Hershey's® Bittersweet Chocolate Bar. This bar was replaced by Hershey's® Semi-Sweet Bar in 1949. Special Dark®, a sweeter dark chocolate, followed in 1971. In 1992, Hershey's introduced a smoother, slightly darker version of Special Dark® that is still sold today.

Butterfinger® Banana Cake with Peanut Butter Cream Cheese Frosting

∼ We kept testing this cake because it was so good. ∼

DIFFICULTY: ▲▲◢

EQUIPMENT: Two 9-inch round cake pans, parchment paper (optional), electric mixer, food processor fitted with a metal blade

FOR THE CAKE

4 Butterfinger® Bars (2.1 oz. bars)
4 ounces butter (1 stick), room temperature
1 ¾ cups sugar
3 eggs
4 very ripe bananas, mashed
1 teaspoon vanilla
2 ½ cups flour
1 teaspoon baking soda
⅛ teaspoon salt
⅔ cup buttermilk

FOR THE FROSTING

12 ounces cream cheese, room temperature
2 ounces butter (½ stick), room temperature
1 teaspoon vanilla
6 cups powdered sugar, sifted
½ cup peanut butter (optional)

MAKE THE CAKE

1. Preheat the oven to 350°. Lightly butter and flour two 9-inch round cake pans. (We also recommend lining cake pans with parchment paper.)

2. In the food processor, coarsely chop the candy bars.

3. In a large bowl, cream together butter and sugar for 1 minute on high. Beat in the eggs one at a time, scraping down the sides of the bowl.

4. Mix in mashed bananas and vanilla.

5. In a separate bowl, combine the flour, baking soda and salt. Add the dry ingredients and the buttermilk alternately to the egg mixture and incorporate thoroughly.

6. Fold in the chopped candy bars and pour the batter evenly into the prepared cake pans.

7. Bake for about 30 minutes, or until toothpick inserted in the center of the cake comes out clean.

8. Cool the cakes for 10 minutes. Invert onto a rack and cool completely before frosting.

Make the Frosting

1. In a large mixing bowl, blend the cream cheese, butter and vanilla on high until smooth, scraping down the sides of the bowl.

2. Add the powdered sugar and peanut butter (if desired) and mix on medium until smooth.

Frost the Cake

1. Place one cake layer on a plate. Spread one-third of the frosting over the top.

2. Place second layer of cake on top. Spread the remaining frosting over the top and sides of the cake. Serves 10.

Mounds® German Chocolate Cake

∞ Even better than traditional German Chocolate Cake. ∞

DIFFICULTY: 🍫🍫

EQUIPMENT: Two 9-inch round cake pans, parchment paper (optional), electric mixer

FOR THE CAKE

4 Mounds® Bars (1.9 oz. bars)
1 box dark chocolate cake mix (18.25 oz.)

FOR THE FROSTING

3 Mounds® Bars (1.9 oz. bars)
1 egg, beaten
1 can evaporated milk (5 oz. can)
¹/₂ cup sugar
¹/₄ cup butter
1 cup flaked coconut
¹/₂ cup pecans, chopped

FOR THE CAKE

1. Preheat the oven to 350°. Butter and flour two 9-inch round cake pans. (We also recommend lining cake pans with parchment paper.)
2. Chop 4 candy bars into ¹/₄-inch pieces. Set aside.
3. Mix the cake as directed on the box.
4. Fold the chopped candy bars into the batter.
5. Pour the batter evenly into prepared cake pans.
6. Bake for 25 to 30 minutes or until a toothpick inserted in the center of the cake comes out clean.
7. Cool cakes in pans for 15 minutes. Invert cakes onto a rack and cool completely before frosting.

FOR THE FROSTING

1. Chop 3 candy bars coarsely and place in a heavy saucepan.
2. Add the beaten egg, evaporated milk, sugar, butter and chopped candy bars. Stir until mixture becomes thick and bubbly, about 12 minutes. Remove from heat.
3. Add the flaked coconut and pecans and stir until well combined.
4. Cool frosting to room temperature.

FROST THE CAKE

1. Place one cake layer on a serving plate. Spread one-third of frosting over the top.
2. Place the second cake layer on top. With the remaining frosting, evenly cover the top and sides of the cake. Serves 10.

MOUNDS®

In 1919 Peter Paul Halajian and five of his friends began selling their homemade chocolate confections door-to-door. Within a few years, they introduced Konabar® and Mounds®, and found a permanent place for their business in Naugatuck, Connecticut. During the war, when sugar and coconut became scarce, they dropped all their candy lines except Mounds®.

No longer able to purchase fresh coconut from the Philippines, they hired ships to transport it from Central America. Since Mounds® was their sole bar, they added a second "Mound" to the package and kept the price at 5 cents. Doing one thing well has made this bar an enduring American favorite. Almond Joy® followed in 1948.

5th Avenue® Pound Cake

∾ Quick and easy to make. ∾

DIFFICULTY: ◆

EQUIPMENT: food processor fitted with a metal blade, electric mixer

FOR THE CAKE

1 prepared pound cake (12 oz. cake)

FOR THE FROSTING

10 5th Avenue® Bars (2 oz. bars)
2 cups whipping cream
2 tablespoons unsweetened cocoa
¹/₄ cup powdered sugar, sifted

PREPARE THE CAKE

1. Slice the frozen pound cake lengthwise into 4 long, thin layers.

MAKE THE FROSTING

1. In the food processor, coarsely chop the candy bars. Set aside ¹/₂ cup for garnish.

2. In a large bowl, using an electric mixer, whip the cream, cocoa and sugar together until stiff peaks form.

3. Fold the chopped candy bars into the whipped cream.

ASSEMBLE THE CAKE

1. Place the bottom layer of the pound cake onto a serving plate. Spread ¹/₄ cup of frosting evenly over the top of this layer.

2. Place the next layer of cake on top and spread ¹/₄ cup frosting evenly over this layer.

3. Repeat the process with the remaining 2 layers of cake.

4. After all 4 layers have been frosted, frost the sides and ends of the cake.

5. Garnish with the remaining chopped candy. Refrigerate until served. Serves 10.

5TH AVENUE®

According to Hershey's archives, William H. Luden started his candy company in his mother's 5 x 6-foot kitchen in Reading, Pennsylvania. His first local candy sensation was a popular brown sugar and molasses candy called "moshie." He also made hand-dipped chocolates, hard candy, marshmallow items, peppermint patties and penny candies. One of Luden's most famous recipes was for honey licorice-flavored cough drops, introduced in 1881, that are still available today. Luden's best-selling 5th Avenue® bar followed some years later in 1936.

Snickers® Cheesecake

⁓ Snickers on steroids. ⁓

DIFFICULTY: ▲▲

EQUIPMENT: 9 or 10-inch spring-form pan, parchment paper (optional), aluminum foil, food processor fitted with a metal blade, drinking glass (as needed), cookie sheet, double boiler, electric mixer

FOR THE CRUST

35 OREO® Chocolate Sandwich Cookies
4 tablespoons butter, melted
2 tablespoons water
¹/₄ cup sugar

FOR THE FILLING

24 ounces cream cheese, room temperature
2 eggs
8 ounces sour cream
1 cup sugar
1 ¹/₂ cups chocolate chips
5 Snickers® Bars (2.07 oz. bars), coarsely chopped

FOR THE CHOCOLATE GLAZE

1 cup semi-sweet chocolate chips
2 tablespoons butter
5 ounces whipping cream

MAKE THE CRUST

1. Preheat the oven to 375°. Wrap the bottom of a 9 or 10-inch spring-form pan tightly with aluminum foil.

2. In the food processor, finely crush the OREO® cookies.

3. Add the melted butter, water and sugar to the cookie crumbs and continue processing until well blended.

4. Press evenly over the bottom and half way up the sides of the pan. Bake for 7 minutes. The crust may rise slightly during baking. Use the flat bottom of a drinking glass to gently press down the crust. Set aside.

MAKE THE FILLING

1. In a large bowl, using an electric mixer, beat the cream cheese until light and fluffy. Beat in eggs, one at a time, scraping down sides of bowl after each addition.

2. Add in the sour cream and sugar.

3. Fold in the chocolate chips and chopped candy bars.

continued on next page

4. Pour the batter into the crust.

5. Place the cheesecake onto a cookie sheet and bake at 375° for about 65 minutes, or until lightly golden. The cheesecake will form a perfect dome—no dip in the center—when it is fully baked. If using a baking thermometer, it should read 160° when done.

6. Transfer to a rack and cool. As cheesecake cools, the domed center will fall below the crust, forming a shallow crater.

7. Lay a piece of plastic wrap directly on top of the cheesecake and refrigerate in pan for 4 hours. Cake may be made 1 or 2 days before serving and kept tightly covered in refrigerator.

MAKE THE CHOCOLATE GLAZE

1. In a double boiler over medium heat, melt the chips and butter with one-third of the cream. Remove from heat and stir until smooth.

2. Stir in remaining cream and mix until thoroughly incorporated.

FINAL ASSEMBLY

1. Run a knife around the edge of the pan to loosen the cheesecake.

2. Release the cheesecake and place it on a serving plate.

3. Pour the glaze into the shallow crater.

4. Refrigerate for 10 minutes to allow the glaze to set. Serves 12.

SNICKERS®

Snickers® has been America's best-selling candy bar since it was first introduced in 1930. But Frank Mars didn't start out on top. He went broke more than once before he invented his signature nougat-filled candy bars. He had so many failures that his first wife left him in 1910 for fear that she and their son Forrest would not be properly fed and clothed.

Success is not always wrapped in good timing, but Frank Mars persevered, testing batches of candy in his own kitchen until he became an industry leader.

Special Dark® Chocolate Torte with Raspberry Topping

⌒ A head-turner and a palette pleaser. ⌒

DIFFICULTY: ♦♦♦

EQUIPMENT: 9-inch round cake pan, parchment paper (optional), strainer, electric mixer, pastry bag with No. 6 (or ¾-inch) tip, whisk

FOR THE TORTE

1 cup all-purpose flour
1 cup sugar
⅓ cup unsweetened cocoa powder
½ teaspoon baking powder
½ teaspoon baking soda
4 ounces butter (1 stick), room temperature
⅓ cup milk
¼ cup water
1 egg
1 teaspoon vanilla

FOR THE WHIPPED RASPBERRY TOPPING

12 ounces frozen raspberries
4 teaspoons cornstarch
2 tablespoons sugar
1 cup whipping cream

FOR THE CHOCOLATE FROSTING

1 large (7 oz.) Hershey's Special Dark® Bar or
  5 (1.45 oz) Bars
2 tablespoons butter
8 ounces whipping cream

MAKE THE TORTE

NOTE: If you have a wire whip attachment for your electric mixer, we recommend using it to mix the cake and topping. If not, use regular beaters.

1. Preheat the oven to 350°. Lightly butter and flour a 9-inch cake pan. (We also recommend lining cake pans with parchment paper.)

2. In a medium bowl, stir together flour, sugar, cocoa powder, baking powder and baking soda. Set aside.

3. In a large bowl, using an electric mixer, whip the butter on high until pale and fluffy. Add the milk, water, egg and vanilla and mix on high for 1 minute.

continued on next page

4. Add the flour mixture to the butter and mix for 1 minute on medium, scraping down the sides. Blend on high for another 3 minutes.

5. Pour the batter evenly into the prepared pan and bake for 25 to 30 minutes, or until a toothpick inserted in the center of the cake comes out clean.

MAKE THE WHIPPED RASPBERRY TOPPING

1. In a heavy saucepan over medium heat, cook raspberries, mashing them gently with a fork or wooden spoon as they heat. Remove from heat.

2. Pour raspberries into strainer set over a large mixing bowl. Strain the raspberries, extracting as much juice as possible. Discard pulp. You should have ³/4 cup of raspberry juice. If you have less, add water to make ³/4 cup.

3. Place ¹/2 cup raspberry juice in a small clean saucepan.

4. In a small bowl, mix together cornstarch and sugar. Pour the remaining ¹/4 cup of raspberry juice into the sugar mixture and stir until smooth.

5. Add this mixture to the raspberry juice in the saucepan. Heat to a boil, stirring constantly. Remove from heat. Cool in the refrigerator for 45 minutes.

6. Spoon the cold raspberry sauce into a large mixing bowl and blend for 10 seconds on high. Add the cream and whip until stiff peaks form. Set aside in refrigerator.

MAKING THE CHOCOLATE FROSTING

1. In a double boiler over medium heat, melt the candy bars and butter, stirring occasionally. Remove from heat as soon as the mixture has melted. Cool completely.

2. In a large mixing bowl, combine the cooled chocolate mixture and one-third of the cream. Whisk until fully incorporated.

3. Place in the refrigerator for 30 minutes.

4. Add the remaining cream and mix on high until stiff peaks form. (This will happen quickly.)

ASSEMBLE THE TORTE

1. Place the cake on a serving plate. Spread the chocolate frosting over the top and sides of the cake, reserving 1 cup of frosting for the border.

2. With a pastry bag, use the remaining cup of frosting, and with a No. 6 tip or ³/4-inch tip, pipe a border around the rim of the cake.

3. Mound the raspberry cream on top of the cake all the way to the edge. Serves 10 to 12.

Chocolate Soufflés with York®
Peppermint Patties Crème Anglaise

∾ Great for dessert, but even better for breakfast... ∾

DIFFICULTY: ♦♦♦
**EQUIPMENT: Four to six 4-inch ramekins,
electric mixer**

FOR THE CRÈME ANGLAISE

NOTE: Make the crème anglaise several
hours or one day ahead and refrigerate.

³/₄ cup milk
12 miniature York® Peppermint Patties
¹/₄ cup sugar

FOR THE CHOCOLATE SOUFFLÉS

4 egg yolks
*4 squares unsweetened baking chocolate (1 oz.
each)*
1 cup milk
³/₄ cup sugar
¹/₂ teaspoon salt
¹/₂ teaspoon vanilla
*3 tablespoons butter (plus additional for butter-
ing ramekins)*
5 tablespoons flour
5 egg whites

2 tablespoons additional sugar
MAKE THE CRÈME ANGLAISE

1. In a heavy saucepan over medium heat,
   melt the York® Peppermint Patties with
   the milk and sugar. Stir until smooth.

2. Remove from heat and cool for 10 minutes. Transfer to a storage container and
   refrigerate until serving.

MAKE THE SOUFFLÉS

1. Preheat the oven to 375°. Generously
   butter the ramekins and coat the insides
   with sugar.

2. Separate 5 eggs. Discard 1 egg yolk. Set
   aside 4 remaining yolks and the egg
   whites in separate bowls.

3. Finely chop the baking chocolate and
   set aside.

4. In a medium bowl, combine the milk, ¹/₂
   cup sugar and salt.

5. In a skillet over medium heat, melt 3
   tablespoons butter and flour together
   and blend to form a roux, or smooth

continued on next page

thick paste.

6. Whisk the milk mixture into the roux. Stir until thick and smooth. Reduce heat to low.

7. Add the chocolate and vanilla. Stir continuously until the chocolate melts.

8. Thoroughly whisk in egg yolks and remove from the burner. Set aside.

9. In a clean, dry mixing bowl with electric mixer, whip the egg whites until foamy.

10. Add 2 tablespoons sugar and whip until the whites form stiff peaks.

11. Add 1 cup of the egg whites to the chocolate mixture (still in skillet) and fold together to loosen the chocolate mixture.

12. Add the chocolate mixture to the remaining eggs whites and gently fold in until completely blended.

13. Fill each prepared ramekin evenly with the batter. Clean any batter from the rims of the ramekins.

14. Bake for 38 to 42 minutes. Serve immediately with chilled crème anglaise.

SERVING SUGGESTION: Using a fancy spoon, let each guest poke a hole in the top of their soufflé and spoon in the cold crème anglaise. Serves 4 to 6.

YORK® PEPPERMINT PATTIES

An ice cream cone manufacturer created York® Peppermint Patties in 1940. The York Cone Company, as they were known, made ice cream cones, waffles and candy in York, Pennsylvania. Their peppermint patties became so popular in the northeast that they ceased making all other types of candy to meet the demand. In 1975, Peter Paul, backed by their first advertising campaign, launched the candies nationwide with "York® Peppermint Pattie: Get the sensation."

C-c-cold Candy Confections

Ice Cream Pies, Cakes, Parfaits and Bon Bons

Nutrageous® Ice Cream Cake

∽ *A total Nutrage.* ∽

DIFFICULTY: ♠♠♠

EQUIPMENT: Three 9-inch round cake pans, parchment paper (optional), food processor fitted with a metal blade, large mixing bowl, electric mixer

FOR THE CAKE

2 boxes Devil's Food cake mix (18.25 oz. each)

FOR THE FILLING

9 Nutrageous® Bars (1.92 oz. bars)
1 pint premium chocolate ice cream, softened 30 minutes in refrigerator
1 pint premium vanilla ice cream, softened 30 minutes in refrigerator
1 can prepared dark chocolate frosting (16 oz. can)
1/2 cup butterscotch chips

FOR THE WHIPPED CREAM FROSTING

2 cups whipping cream
1 cup powdered sugar, sifted
1/2 teaspoon vanilla

MAKE THE CAKES

1. Preheat the oven to 350°. Lightly butter and flour three 9-inch cake pans. (We also recommend lining cake pans with parchment paper.)

2. *This step yields 3 cake layers.* Prepare both cake mixes in one large mixing bowl. Add all ingredients listed on each box.

3. Pour 3 cups of batter into each of the prepared cake pans.

4. Bake for 28 to 30 minutes, or until a toothpick inserted in the center of the cake comes out clean.

5. Remove cakes and cool for 10 minutes. Invert cakes onto a rack. (If you only have 2 cake pans, wash 1 of the pans and lightly butter and flour the bottom. Pour the remaining batter into the prepared pan and bake for 28 to 30 minutes.)

6. Cool cakes completely before proceeding, or freeze until needed.

MAKE THE FILLING

1. Freeze the Nutrageous® Bars for 30 minutes.
2. In the food processor, coarsely chop the frozen candy bars. Divide the chopped candy into 2 medium bowls. In one bowl mix together the vanilla ice cream and chopped candy. In the other bowl mix together the chocolate ice cream and chopped candy. Set aside in freezer until needed.

ASSEMBLE THE CAKE

1. Place one of the cooled cake layers on a plate.
2. Spread one-half of the chocolate icing on top of the first layer of cake. Sprinkle ¼ cup of butterscotch chips evenly over chocolate icing. Spread the chocolate ice cream mixture over the chips.
3. Place the next cake layer on top and cover with the remaining chocolate icing. Sprinkle the remaining butterscotch chips on top, then spread the vanilla ice cream mixture over the chips.
4. Place the third cake layer on top of vanilla layer.
5. Cover loosely and freeze the cake for at least 1 hour before frosting as below.

MAKE THE WHIPPED CREAM FROSTING

1. In a large mixing bowl, combine the cream, powdered sugar and vanilla. Beat until stiff peaks form.
2. Remove cake from freezer and spread whipped cream frosting evenly over top and sides of the cake. Freeze at least 1 hour before serving. Serves 12 to 14.

NUTRAGEOUS®

The H. B. Reese Candy Co., a division of Hershey's, introduced the Nutrageous® bar in 1993. It gets its name from the loads of peanuts throughout and a very peanut-buttery center.

Junior Mints® Parfait
∽ *Yum, yum and double yum!* ∽

DIFFICULTY: ●
EQUIPMENT: 4 to 6 parfait glasses or tall
glass tumblers, electric mixer

FOR THE PARFAIT

1 box brownie mix (19.8 oz. box)
2 cups chocolate sauce
1 pint of premium vanilla ice cream, softened
  10 minutes in refrigerator
2 boxes of Junior Mints® (1.84 oz. boxes)

FOR THE WHIPPED CREAM TOPPING

1 cup whipping cream
¹/₄ cup powdered sugar, sifted
¹/₂ teaspoon vanilla

MAKE THE BROWNIES

1. Prepare and bake the brownies as directed
   on the box.
2. Cool completely and cut into eighteen
   2-inch squares.

MAKE THE WHIPPED CREAM TOPPING

1. In a medium mixing bowl using electric
   mixer, combine the cream, powdered
   sugar and vanilla. Beat until stiff peaks
   form. Set aside for assembly.

ASSEMBLE THE PARFAIT

2. Place a brownie square in the bottom of
   a parfait glass or tumbler.
3. Sprinkle 2 or 3 Junior Mints® on top of
   the brownie.
4. Place a small scoop of ice cream on top
   of the mints.
5. Pour a small ribbon of chocolate sauce on
   top of the ice cream.
6. Sprinkle 2 or 3 Junior Mints® on top of
   the sauce.
7. Repeat the process until you reach the
   top of the parfait glass. Garnish with
   whipped cream and Junior Mints®.
   Makes at least 6 parfaits.

JUNIOR MINTS®

Most Americans think the name Junior Mints® refers to this candy's small size, but the name is actually a play on words. The name Junior Mints® comes from the 1941 Broadway hit *Junior Miss*. The story involved the ups and downs of a teenage debutante as she came of age. When James Welch debuted his Junior Mints® in 1949, he introduced them to the American public in much the same way a debutante is introduced to society. Even his advertisements read like a society page announcement. Junior Mints® have been the talk of the town ever since.

Caramel Skor® Ice Cream Pie

∾ Skor® pie is so good, it's skary. ∾

DIFFICULTY: 🍫🍫
EQUIPMENT: 9-inch pie pan, food processor fitted with a metal blade, drinking glass (as needed), large spoon

FOR THE CRUST

14 OREO® Chocolate Sandwich Cookies
4 tablespoons butter, melted

FOR THE FILLING

2 pints premium caramel swirl ice cream,
  softened 30 minutes in refrigerator
6 Skor® Bars (1.4 oz. bars)

FOR THE CHOCOLATE TOPPING

4 Skor® Bars (1.4 oz. bars)
1 tablespoon butter
2 ounces of whipping cream

MAKE THE CRUST

1. Preheat the oven to 375°.
2. In the food processor, finely crush the OREO® cookies. Add the melted butter to the cookie crumbs and continue processing until well blended.
3. Transfer the mixture to pie pan and press evenly over the bottom and up the sides of the pan.
4. Bake for 10 minutes. The crust may rise slightly during baking. Use the flat bottom of a drinking glass to gently press down the crust. Cool completely before filling.

MAKE THE FILLING

1. In the food processor, finely chop the candy bars.
2. Place the ice cream in a large mixing bowl.
3. Stir the chopped candy bars and ice cream together.
4. Spoon the ice cream into the cooled piecrust.

5. Using the back of a large spoon, form a shallow crater in the center of the ice cream, leaving a 1-inch border around the edge. This crater will hold the chocolate topping, leaving an ice cream border.

6. Place the pie in the freezer for 30 minutes.

MAKE THE CHOCOLATE TOPPING

1. In a food processor, finely crush the remaining four candy bars.

2. In a heavy saucepan over medium heat, melt butter and crushed candy bars with the cream. Stir until melted and well blended. The mixture may contain bits of unmelted toffee.

3. Remove from heat. Cool to room temperature.

4. Remove frozen pie from freezer and fill the ice cream crater with the chocolate topping.

5. Freeze 10 minutes before serving. Serves 8 to 10.

SKOR®

Hershey's came out with Skor®, a slightly more buttery-flavored toffee than its competitor Heath®, in 1982. Today Hershey's owns both Skor® and Heath®.

Peppermint Ice Cream Puffs

~ This dessert is a Christmas Eve tradition in Alison's family. ~

DIFFICULTY: ▲▲▲

EQUIPMENT: whisk, parchment paper, cookie sheet, electric mixer, pastry brush, double boiler, food processor fitted with metal blade

NOTE: Puffs can be made ahead and frozen.

FOR THE PUFFS

¾ cup water
6 tablespoons butter
1½ teaspoons sugar
⅛ teaspoon salt
¾ cup all-purpose flour
2 eggs, plus 1 egg for egg wash

FOR THE FILLING

1 quart premium vanilla ice cream, softened 30 minutes in refrigerator
30 peppermint candy disks
1¼ teaspoons peppermint extract

FOR THE CHOCOLATE SAUCE

1 cup semi-sweet chocolate chips
2 tablespoons butter
5 ounces whipping cream

MAKE THE PUFFS

1. Preheat the oven to 400°. Line a baking sheet with parchment paper.

2. In a heavy saucepan over medium heat, bring the water, butter, sugar and salt to a boil, stirring occasionally. Remove pan from heat and gradually whisk in the flour.

3. Return to burner, whisking vigorously over medium heat until the dough pulls away from the sides of the pan and begins to form a ball. Cool for 10 minutes.

4. Transfer dough to a large mixing bowl. With electric mixer running, beat 3 eggs into the dough. Scrape down the sides of the bowl after each egg.

5. Drop 1½-inch mounds of dough onto the parchment-lined cookie sheet, spacing 2 inches apart (or transfer the dough to a

continued on next page

pastry bag, fitted with ½-inch tip and pipe the 1½-inch mounds).

6. In a small bowl, beat the remaining egg. Brush the tops of the dough mounds with the beaten egg.

7. Bake for 20 minutes at 400°. Reduce heat to 350° and bake until golden brown, about 15 minutes. Cool completely on racks. Puffs can be made ahead and frozen in an airtight container.

MAKE THE FILLING

1. In the food processor, finely crush the peppermint candy. Set aside ½ cup for garnish.

2. In a large bowl, mix the crushed candy and peppermint extract into the ice cream. Set aside in the freezer.

MAKE THE CHOCOLATE SAUCE

1. In a double boiler over medium heat, melt the chips and butter with one-third of the cream stirring often.

2. Remove from heat and stir until smooth.

3. Stir in the remaining cream and mix until thoroughly incorporated. Cool for 10 minutes.

ASSEMBLE THE ICE CREAM PUFFS

1. Slice each puff in half, like a sandwich roll.

2. Set 2 puff bottoms on each serving plate. Place a scoop of peppermint ice cream on each.

3. Cover with a puff top and spoon warm chocolate sauce on top and garnish with crushed peppermint candies. Serves 8.

100 Grand® Ice Cream Nuggets Dipped in Chocolate

∾ A grand little treat. ∾

DIFFICULTY: 🌰🌰

EQUIPMENT: food processor fitted with a metal blade, small ice cream scoop or melon-baller, wire rack, cookie sheet

FOR THE CHOCOLATE COATING

1 1/2 cups semisweet chocolate chips
2 tablespoons canola oil

FOR THE COOKIE COATING

16 OREO® Chocolate Sandwich Cookies

FOR THE FILLING

6 100 Grand® Bars (1.5 oz. bars), frozen 30 minutes
1 pint premium vanilla ice cream, softened 30 minutes in refrigerator

MAKE THE CHOCOLATE COATING

1. In a heavy saucepan over low heat, melt the chocolate chips with the oil and stir until smooth. Remove from heat and cool to room temperature.

MAKE THE COOKIE COATING

1. In the food processor, finely crush the OREO® cookies. Transfer to a medium bowl and set aside.

MAKE THE FILLING

1. Coarsely chop the frozen candy bars in the food processor.
2. Transfer the softened ice cream into a large bowl. Stir in the chopped candy.
3. Place the ice cream mixture in freezer for 10 minutes.
4. Using a small ice cream scoop or melon-baller, scoop out 18 1 1/2-inch ice cream nuggets.

continued on next page

5. Roll each nugget in the cookie crumbs. Transfer onto a plate and freeze for 30 minutes.

6. Place the cookie-coated ice cream nuggets onto a rack set over a cookie sheet, spacing 2 inches apart.

7. Spoon the melted chocolate over each nugget. Allow chocolate to set 5 minutes.

8. Transfer nuggets to a plate and freeze for at least 1 hour before serving. Makes 18 ice cream nuggets.

100 GRAND®

Nestlé introduced the 100 Grand® Bar in 1966. According to candy historian Ray Broekel, the name 100 Grand® came from a 1950's quiz show called *The Big Surprise*. Contestants had to answer 10 questions, worth between $100 and $100,000. Nestlé named their new bar after the 100 Grand® jackpot. The six-figure dollar sign used to be printed across the wrapper like prize money. Today it's simply called 100 Grand®.

Almond Roca® Buttercrunch Ice Cream Tart

∼ Elegant, easy-to-make and the perfect ending to any dinner party. ∼

DIFFICULTY: ♦♦

EQUIPMENT: 10-inch fluted tart pan with a removable bottom or a 9-inch pie pan, food processor fitted with a metal blade

FOR THE CRUST

1 1/2 cups sliced almonds
25 OREO® Chocolate Sandwich Cookies
2 ounces butter, melted (1/2 stick)

FOR THE FILLING

3 cups (about 40 pieces) Almond Roca®
*   Buttercrunch*
2 pints premium coffee ice cream, softened 30
*   minutes in refrigerator*

MAKE THE CRUST

1. Preheat the oven to 350°.
2. Spread sliced almonds in a shallow pan and toast for 10 minutes. Cool and set aside 1/2 cup for topping.
3. In the food processor, finely crush the OREO® cookies and 1 cup of toasted almonds.

4. Add melted butter and pulse until the mixture is well blended.
5. Press the cookie crumb mixture into the bottom of a 10-inch tart pan (or 9-inch pie pan) and up the sides.
6. Freeze crust for 45 minutes.

MAKE THE FILLING

1. Coarsely chop Almond Roca® Buttercrunch. Set aside 1 cup for topping.
2. In a large bowl, combine 2 cups chopped candy and ice cream, and stir well.
3. Transfer filling to the prepared crust and spread evenly. Set aside in freezer.

MAKE THE TOPPING

1. Sprinkle 1/2 cup of reserved toasted almonds and 1 cup of reserved Almond Roca® Buttercrunch pieces evenly over the top of tart.
2. Cover the ice cream tart with plastic wrap and freeze for at least 1 hour or overnight before serving. Serves 10 to 12.

ALMOND ROCA® BUTTERCRUNCH

In 1923 Harry Brown and J. C. Haley invented a crunchy toffee log dipped in chocolate and rolled in finely chopped almonds. They wanted to give their new confection a clever name, something that would really catch on. A local Tacoma librarian suggested the name *roca*, the Spanish word for rock. This term was fitting, since most almonds at that time were imported from Spain. After Brown & Haley found the name, they had to find a way to keep their candy fresh on store shelves. An ordinary coffee can was the original inspiration for their now-famous pink tin.

After Eight® Ice Cream Roll

⁓ Before or after eight, this is a real treat. ⁓

DIFFICULTY: ♦♦♦
EQUIPMENT: 15 x 10-inch jelly roll pan, double boiler, clean dish towel

FOR THE CAKE

¹/₂ cup flour
¹/₃ cup unsweetened cocoa
¹/₄ cup sugar
¹/₂ teaspoon baking soda
¹/₄ teaspoon salt
3 eggs
¹/₂ cup additional sugar
1 teaspoon vanilla
¹/₃ cup water
1 tablespoon additional sugar (to mix with egg whites)

FOR THE FILLING

1 box After Eight® Mints (8.75 oz. box), frozen
1 quart premium vanilla ice cream, softened 30 minutes in refrigerator

FOR THE CHOCOLATE GLAZE

1 cup semi-sweet chocolate chips
2 tablespoons butter
3 ounces whipping cream

MAKE THE CAKE

1. Preheat the oven to 350°.

2. Line a 15 x 10-inch jelly roll pan with aluminum foil and spray surface with nonstick spray.

3. Separate 3 eggs and set aside.

4. In a small bowl, combine the flour, cocoa, ¹/₄ cup of sugar, baking soda and salt. Set aside.

5. In a large mixing bowl, using electric mixer, beat the egg yolks on high until light yellow and fluffy, about 3 minutes.

6. Gradually add ¹/₂ cup of sugar and vanilla and continue to beat on high for 2 minutes.

7. Mix in the flour mixture and water alternately on low, until the batter is smooth. Set aside.

continued on next page

8. In a clean, dry medium bowl, beat the egg whites until foamy.

9. Add 1 tablespoon of sugar and continue to beat until stiff peaks form.

10. Gently fold the egg whites into the batter until combined.

11. Spread the batter evenly into prepared jelly roll pan.

12. Bake 14 to 16 minutes or until a toothpick inserted in the center comes out clean.

13. Just before cake is done, soak a clean dishtowel in water, wring it out thoroughly and lay it on a flat surface.

14. When cake is done, remove from oven and immediately invert the cake onto the dampened dishtowel. Remove the jelly roll pan and very gently roll the cake, foil and towel together, like a sleeping bag.

15. Allow cake to rest as rolled for 1 minute.

16. Gently unroll the cake and peel away the foil, being careful not to tear cake.

17. Reroll the cake (without towel) and gently move to a rack to cool completely.

MAKE THE FILLING

1. Coarsely chop the frozen After Eight® Mints into $1/4$-inch pieces and place in a large mixing bowl.

2. Add softened ice cream and stir together.

3. Place in freezer until final assembly.

ASSEMBLE THE ICE CREAM ROLL

1. Remove prepared ice cream from freezer.

2. Gently unroll the cake.

3. Spread the ice cream evenly over the surface of the cake, leaving a 1-inch border on all sides.

4. Reroll the cake and ice cream like a sleeping bag.

5. Wrap roll tightly with plastic wrap and store in the freezer until ready to glaze.

MAKE THE CHOCOLATE GLAZE

NOTE: Make the glaze just before serving the cake.

1. In a double boiler over medium heat, melt the chips, butter and one-third of the cream stirring often.

2. Remove from heat and stir until smooth.

3. Add the remaining cream and stir until combined.

GLAZE THE CAKE

1. Place the cake on a serving platter.
2. Slowly pour the glaze over the top of the ice cream roll, allowing it to run down the sides. Serve immediately. Serves 12 to 14.

AFTER EIGHT®

After Eight® Mints debuted in Scotland in 1962 and came to America in the late 1960's.
The idea for the name originated with the traditional dinner party. Dinner is typically over
by eight o'clock, so guests are ready for coffee and mints anytime thereafter.

Heath® Bar Ice Cream Sandwiches

⁓ Extraordinary ice cream sandwiches. ⁓

DIFFICULTY: ▲▲▲

EQUIPMENT: food processor fitted with a metal blade, 13 x 9-inch pan, electric mixer, plastic wrap, cookie sheet, rolling pin, sharp knife or pizza cutter

FOR THE FILLING

*1 quart premium vanilla ice cream, softened 20
  minutes in refrigerator*
6 Heath® Bars (1.4 oz. bars), about 1¹/₂ cups

FOR THE CHOCOLATE COOKIE

6 ounces butter (1¹/₂ sticks) room temperature
¹/₂ cup sugar
1 egg yolk
¹/₂ teaspoon vanilla
1¹/₄ cups flour
¹/₄ cup unsweetened cocoa

MAKE THE FILLING

1. Line a 13 x 9-inch cake pan with plastic wrap.

2. In the food processor, coarsely chop the candy bars.

3. Place the softened ice cream in a bowl and mix in the chopped candy.

4. Spoon the ice cream mixture into the lined pan.

5. Cover the ice cream and pan with another layer of plastic wrap.

6. Press the ice cream flat and level, to fill the pan evenly. The ice cream will be about ¹/₂-inch thick. Place in freezer and allow to harden completely before assembling ice cream sandwiches—at least 2 hours.

MAKE THE COOKIES

1. In a large mixing bowl, using an electric mixer, cream together butter, sugar, egg yolk and vanilla.

2. Mix in the flour and cocoa until mixture comes together and dough forms.

3. Transfer the dough onto a large piece of plastic wrap. Place another piece of plastic wrap on top of the dough and roll the dough into a 9 x 12-inch rectangle. The dough should be ¹/₄-inch thick.

continued on next page

4. Transfer dough to a cookie sheet and chill for 30 minutes.

5. Preheat the oven to 375° and prepare a clean cookie sheet with nonstick cooking spray.

6. Remove the cold dough from the refrigerator and peel off the top sheet of plastic wrap.

7. Invert the cold dough onto prepared cookie sheet and peel off remaining piece of plastic wrap.

8. With a knife or a pizza cutter, cut the dough into twelve 3-inch squares. Leave the pieces in place.

9. Bake until cookies are firm to touch, about 20 minutes.

10. Remove from oven and, following the lines from previous cut, recut the cookies and separate slightly.

11. Allow to cool 10 minutes before transferring cookies to a rack to cool completely before assembling.

ASSEMBLE THE ICE CREAM SANDWICHES

1. Place a serving plate in the freezer.

2. Lay 12 cookie squares on a clean surface.

3. Place the uncovered pan of prepared ice cream nearby.

4. Cut a square of ice cream and place it on top of a cookie.

5. Place a cookie top over ice cream and immediately place sandwich on the plate in the freezer. Repeat with the remaining cookies.

6. Cover the ice cream sandwiches with plastic wrap until ready to serve. Makes 6 sandwiches.

HEATH® BAR

According to Hershey's archives, a schoolteacher named L. S. Heath helped his sons Bayard and Everett establish a soda fountain, ice cream and candy business in 1914. When the business became successful, L. S. Heath left teaching to work with his sons full-time. In the back of their store in Robinson, Illinois, the boys stirred kettles of toffee with wooden oars. The toffee was cut into rectangular pieces on marble slabs and dipped in milk chocolate. In 1928, they often delivered Heath® bars with milk orders.

Candy Bar Milk Shakes

～ Killer milk shakes. ～

DIFFICULTY: 🌰
EQUIPMENT: food processor fitted with a metal blade or blender

FOR THE MILK SHAKES

3 ounces of chopped candy bar
¹/₂ pint premium ice cream
¹/₄ cup chocolate syrup, or flavor of choice
³/₄ cup milk

MAKE THE MILK SHAKES

1. In the food processor or blender, chop the candy into small pieces.

2. Add ice cream, syrup and milk.

3. Blend to desired thickness. For a thicker shake, reduce the milk by 2 or 3 tablespoons.

4. Pour the shake into a favorite glass.

5. Garnish with chopped candy bar pieces. Makes 1 20 oz. shake.

GREAT CANDY BAR MILK SHAKE COMBINATIONS

NOTE: Freezing the candy bars before processing makes them easy to chop.

Chocolate Ice Cream
Hershey's® Cookies 'n' Mint Nuggets™
M&M's®
Reese's® Peanut Butter Cups® or Reese's Bites®
Mounds®
Junior Mints®
3 Musketeers®

Vanilla Ice Cream
Clark® Bar
Snickers®
Heath® Bar
Almond Joy®
100 Grand®
Nutrageous®
Hershey's® Cookies 'n' Crème Nuggets™
Twix® Bars

continued on next page

Pay Day®
Milky Way®
Brach's Star Bright® Peppermints
After Eight® Mints
Caramello®
Nestlé Crunch®
Skor®

Coffee Ice Cream
Heath® Bar
Hershey's® Special Dark®

CLARK® BAR

According to candy historian Ray Broekel, David L. Clark began his candy operation in 1886. Mr. Clark originally introduced the Clark® Bar in 1917 for American soldiers serving in World War I. In 1930 he presented another popular bar called Zagnut®. He was also known for a line of chewing gums created in the 1930's, including his unusual Teaberry® flavored gum.

Banana Mousse with Twix® Dipping Sticks

Excellent banana flavor and the Twix® Bar dipping sticks give it a gratifying crunch.

DIFFICULTY: ▲▲▲
EQUIPMENT: Four old-fashioned glasses, parfait glasses or coffee mugs electric mixer, food processor fitted with a metal blade

FOR THE MOUSSE

4 egg whites (Note: pasteurized egg whites are available in most grocery stores.)
1½ cups sugar
¼ cup water
1 packet unflavored gelatin
3 ripe bananas
2 teaspoons banana extract
1½ cups whipping cream
8 Twix® Bars

MAKE THE MOUSSE

1. In a large metal mixing bowl, whip the egg whites and sugar until glossy and stiff peaks form. Set aside.

2. In a small glass dish, combine the water and gelatin. Let it stand for 5 minutes.

3. Microwave gelatin mixture on high for 40 seconds. Stir until smooth.

4. In the food processor, purée the bananas. Add the banana extract and gelatin, and process until smooth.

5. Add the banana mixture to the egg white mixture and gently fold together until fully incorporated.

6. In clean dry bowl, whip the cream until it forms stiff peaks. Add the whipped cream to the banana mixture and fold together. Cover with plastic wrap. Refrigerate for 2 hours.

7. Spoon the chilled mousse evenly into each glass.

8. Insert 2 Twix® Bars into the mousse at an angle.

9. Refrigerate until ready to serve. Serves 4.

Use the Twix® Bars as edible spoons with the mousse.

TWIX® BAR

Long lines of uniform dough, like cookie snakes, zoom through an oven tunnel on steel conveyor belts. A swift, continuous ribbon of caramel comes to rest on top as the cookie strips roll on. In automated rhythm the cookies are sliced into snack-sized sticks. Then a billowing wall of chocolate drapes itself over cookie sticks as they whiz by. A wheel underneath the belt spins chocolate onto the bottom of the cookies. The bars are then cooled, wrapped and boxed for shipping. Twix® Cookie Bars debuted on the American market in 1977.

Good Morning, Candy Bars!

⊸ Coffee Cake, Waffles, Muffins and More ⊸

Almond Roca® Buttercrunch Coffee Cake

*⌒ Crumbly toffee streusel and icing make this moist
coffee cake the best we've ever tasted. ⌒*

DIFFICULTY: 🌢🌢
**EQUIPMENT: 10-inch nonstick bundt pan,
food processor fitted with metal blade, electric
mixer**

FOR THE STREUSEL TOPPING

16 pieces Almond Roca® Buttercrunch
¹/₄ cup brown sugar
¹/₂ teaspoon ground cinnamon
¹/₄ cup all-purpose flour
2 tablespoons butter, melted

FOR THE CAKE

4 ounces butter (1 stick), room temperature
¹/₂ cup sugar
¹/₂ cup brown sugar
3 eggs
1 cup sour cream
1 teaspoon almond extract
2 ¹/₂ cups all-purpose flour
1 teaspoon baking powder
1 teaspoon baking soda
¹/₂ teaspoon salt

FOR THE GLAZE

3 cups powdered sugar, sifted
1 tablespoon brown sugar
2 tablespoons butter, melted
3 tablespoons plus 2 teaspoons water
¹/₂ teaspoon almond extract

MAKE THE STREUSEL TOPPING

1. In the food processor, finely chop the
   Almond Roca® Buttercrunch. Set aside
   half of the crushed candy for the cake.

2. To the remaining candy in the food
   processor, add the brown sugar, cinnamon
   and flour. Pulse 3 times to mix together.

3. Add the melted butter and process
   thoroughly. Streusel will have a crumbly
   appearance. Set aside.

MAKE THE COFFEE CAKE

1. Spray the bundt pan evenly with nonstick
   cooking spray and set aside.

continued on next page

2. In a medium bowl using electric mixer, cream together butter, sugar and brown sugar. Add eggs, blending until batter lightens in color, about 2 minutes on medium speed. Scrape down the sides of bowl.

3. Mix in the the sour cream, almond extract, and remaining Almond Roca® Buttercrunch. Mix for 1 minute on low.

4. Add the flour, baking powder, baking soda and salt. Blend until just combined.

5. Pour half of the batter into the bundt pan. Sprinkle half the streusel evenly on top of the batter. Add the remaining batter and top with the rest of the streusel.

6. Bake on the center rack for 45-50 minutes or until a toothpick inserted in the center comes out clean.

7. Cool for 30 minutes. Loosen cake by running a knife around the edge of the pan and invert onto a serving plate to completely cool.

GLAZE THE CAKE

1. In a large bowl, whisk together powdered sugar, brown sugar, melted butter, water and almond extract until smooth.

2. Pour glaze along the ridge of the cake, letting it run down the sides. Serves 10 to 12.

ALMOND ROCA® BUTTERCRUNCH

Americans have enjoyed Almond Roca® since Brown & Haley first introduced it in 1923. Since it is packaged in tins, it was easy to send to American troops during World War II. The soldiers loved Almond Roca®. One time, according to company history, American commanders would not release an occupied territory to the Allies until they had 3 railroad cars filled with Almond Roca® safely in their possession! Today this candy is enjoyed worldwide and has been a favorite with celebrities such as Beverly Sills and Shirley MacLaine.

Milky Way® Pain Au Chocolat

∽ Out of this galaxy! And easy to make. ∽

DIFFICULTY: 🍫
EQUIPMENT: 1 cookie sheet, double boiler

FOR THE PAIN AU CHOCOLAT

2 Milky Way® Bars (2.05 oz. bars)
1 container Pillsbury® Crescent Rolls

FOR THE GLAZE

1/2 cup chocolate chips
1 tablespoon milk
1 tablespoon butter

MAKE THE PAIN AU CHOCOLAT

1. Preheat the oven to 375° and spray a cookie sheet with nonstick spray.

2. Chop the candy bars into 1/4-inch slices.

3. Break open the crescent roll container. The dough will be in 2 halves. Unroll dough and divide on the middle partition, taking care not to tear the diagonal perforations. There will be 4 rectangles of dough.

4. Place all 4 rectangles of dough on the cookie sheet with the narrower edges toward you.

5. Sprinkle 1/4 cup of chopped candy bars on top of each rectangle, leaving a 1/2-inch border on both sides and a 1-inch border on the end furthest from you.

6. Roll up the dough like a sleeping bag, beginning with the edge closest to you. If the diagonal perforations tear when rolling, gently pinch them together.

7. Repeat with the remaining 3 rectangles.

8. Space the pains au chocolat 2 to 3 inches apart.

9. Bake 20 to 22 minutes, or until golden.

MAKE THE CHOCOLATE GLAZE

1. In a double boiler over medium heat, melt the chocolate chips, butter and milk, and stir until smooth.

GLAZE THE PAIN AU CHOCOLAT

1. Drizzle over the pain au chocolat and serve warm. Serves 4.

Raisinets® Granola

This was a favorite with guests at Ric's family's Hawaiian bed-and-breakfast.

DIFFICULTY: 🌢🌢
EQUIPMENT: Blender or food processor fitted with a metal blade, 15 x 10-inch jelly roll pan

FOR THE GRANOLA

3 ¹/₂ cups old-fashioned rolled oats
¹/₂ cup honey
¹/₄ cup canola oil
2 tablespoons water
²/₃ cup shredded coconut
¹/₃ cup chopped dried papaya
¹/₃ cup chopped dried pineapple
¹/₃ cup coarsely chopped macadamia nuts
¹/₂ cup Raisinets®

MAKE THE GRANOLA

1. Preheat the oven to 300°.

2. Place the oats in a large bowl and set aside.

3. Combine the honey, oil and water in a small glass dish and heat for 50 seconds on high in microwave, or heat in a small heavy saucepan over medium until mixture just begins to simmer.

4. Transfer the honey mixture, together with the coconut, into a blender or food processor. Blend for 20 seconds, or until coconut is finely chopped. Pour the coconut mixture over oats and stir until well coated.

5. Spread the oat mixture evenly over the bottom of 15 x 10-inch jelly roll pan and bake for 35 minutes.

6. With a spatula or spoon, turn the oat mixture over a few times and spread it out evenly again.

7. Bake for another 30 minutes. Cool completely.

8. While the granola is cooling, chop the fruit and nuts into ¹/₄-inch chucks.

9. Mix the chopped fruit, nuts, and Raisinets® into the granola. Makes 5 ¹/₂ cups of granola.

GRANOLA

Dr. James Caleb Jackson invented the first breakfast cereal in 1863 and called it *Granula*. His patients couldn't chew these dense bran nuggets unless they soaked them in water for hours. Another doctor, Dr. John Kellogg, soon invented a chewable bran flake called *Granose*. After a stay in one of his sanatoriums, Charles Post recognized the possibilities of "health" foods and went on to invent Postum® and Grape Nuts®. Kellogg's brother soon came out with corn flakes and started another booming cereal business.

Hershey's® Milk Chocolate Popovers

Chocolate popovers with a dab of butter and the morning paper. Mmmm.

DIFFICULTY: 🔸

EQUIPMENT: 1 popover pan or large muffin pan

FOR THE POPOVERS

1 tablespoon butter
4 Hershey's® Milk Chocolate Bars (1.45 oz.
 bars), broken into small pieces
1½ cups milk
3 eggs
½ teaspoon vanilla
1 cup all-purpose flour
¼ teaspoon salt
additional softened butter for pan

MAKE THE POPOVERS

1 Preheat oven to 400°. Place the empty popover pan or muffin pan in the pre-heating oven.

2 In a heavy saucepan over low heat, melt the butter, candy bars and ½ cup of milk. Stir until smooth. Remove the chocolate from heat and cool for 5 minutes.

3 In a large bowl, whisk together the eggs, vanilla, 1 cup of milk, flour and salt until smooth.

4 Stir in the chocolate mixture and mix well.

5 Remove popover pan from oven and put ⅛ teaspoon of butter in each cup.

6 Immediately fill each cup ¾ full with batter.

7 Bake 37 to 40 minutes until popovers rise and begin to brown.

8 Serve immediately with butter. Makes 6 to 8 popovers.

HERSHEY'S® MILK CHOCOLATE

Milton Hershey invented the Hershey's® Milk Chocolate bar in 1894. He opened his first chocolate factory in his hometown, a small Pennsylvania dairy town called Derry Church, because he wanted to have fresh milk on hand to make his chocolate. Over the years, Hershey's® chocolate has become an American tradition. It fueled Admiral Bird's epic expeditions to Antarctica as well as American soldiers in World War II. During the Persian Gulf War, Hershey's even created a special non-melting chocolate bar for the American troops called Desert Bar®.

Symphony® Cinnamon Twists

∼ *Alison's favorite breakfast.* ∼

DIFFICULTY: ♦♦♦

EQUIPMENT: flour for kneading, rolling pin, cookie sheet, food processor fitted with a metal blade, large cutting board, sharp knife

FOR THE DOUGH

1 package active dry yeast (.25 oz. packet), or
  2 1/4 teaspoons
1 cup warm milk
1 egg
1/4 cup butter
1/2 cup sugar
1 teaspoon salt
3 1/2 to 4 cups all-purpose flour

FOR THE FILLING

4 Hershey's® Symphony® Creamy Milk
  Chocolate with Almonds & Toffee Chips
  (1.5 oz. bars)
1/2 cup sugar
1 tablespoon ground cinnamon
2 ounces butter, softened (1/2 stick)

FOR THE GLAZE

2 1/2 cups powdered sugar, sifted

1/4 teaspoon vanilla
2 tablespoons milk

MAKE THE DOUGH

1. In a large bowl, sprinkle the yeast over the warm milk. Stir and let stand for five minutes.

2. Add the egg, butter, sugar and salt and mix until well blended.

3. Gradually add the flour and mix until dough forms.

4. Transfer dough to a lightly floured surface and knead for 15 minutes.

5. Place dough in a large bowl, cover loosely with plastic wrap and let rise in a warm place until doubled in bulk, about 45 minutes. (The dough can also be made in a bread machine as per manufacturer's instructions.)

MAKE THE FILLING

1. While the dough is rising, finely chop the candy bars in the food processor.

continued on next page

2. Add the sugar and cinnamon and pulse until well blended.

MAKE THE TWISTS

1. Preheat the oven to 400°. Spray a cookie sheet with nonstick spray.

2. Punch down the dough and turn it out onto a lightly floured surface. Shape the dough into a rectangle. Roll it into a 23 x 15-inch rectangle about ¼-inch thick. If dough is difficult to roll, let it rest 5 minutes and resume rolling.

3. Rub the softened butter over the entire surface of the dough. Picture the dough as an opened book and sprinkle the chocolate bar mixture evenly and liberally on the left-hand page. Fold the right-hand page over the left-hand page and stretch slightly so the ends are aligned. The "book" is now closed.

4. Carefully transfer the dough onto a large cutting board and turn it so the spine of the "book" is away from you. Pat the dough lightly together to remove any air bubbles.

5. Place the prepared cookie sheet nearby and, beginning at the left-hand side of the dough (with the spine edge facing away), slice the dough into 1-inch wide strips.

6. One at a time, carefully twist each strip of dough 4 or 5 times. (Don't worry if some of the filling spills during the twisting process.)

7. Place each twist on the prepared cookie sheet. Pinch the open ends of the twists together and tuck under.

8. Bake for 14 to 16 minutes or until golden.

MAKE THE GLAZE

1. Combine the powdered sugar with the vanilla and milk, and stir until thick enough to drizzle.

2. Using a small spoon, drizzle glaze evenly over tops of warm twists. Makes 12 to 14 twists, about 10 to 12 inches in length.

These freeze well. Thaw completely before reheating.

SYMPHONY®

Hershey® debuted Symphony® Creamy Milk Chocolate and Symphony® Creamy Milk Chocolate with Almonds & Toffee Chips in 1989. The name was given to suggest a smooth, harmonious blend of flavors and to imply that it is a chocolate for refined tastes.

Cappuccino Muffins with Skor® Bars

⤳ This muffin gets a Skor® of 10. ⤳

DIFFICULTY: 🌑🌑

EQUIPMENT: food processor fitted with a metal blade, electric mixer, 2 muffin pans, paper baking cups

FOR THE MUFFINS

5 Skor® Bars (1.4 oz. bars)
2 eggs
¹/₂ cup canola oil
¹/₂ cup sugar
2¹/₂ teaspoons instant espresso
2¹/₂ teaspoons ground cinnamon
¹/₂ cup milk
2 cups all-purpose flour
2 teaspoons baking soda
1 teaspoon baking powder
¹/₈ teaspoon salt
¹/₂ cup chocolate chips

MAKE THE MUFFINS

1. Preheat the oven to 350°. Line muffin pans with paper baking cups.

2. In the food processor, chop the candy bars into ¹/₄-inch pieces. Set aside ¹/₂ cup for topping.

3. In a large bowl using electric mixer, cream the eggs, oil, sugar, instant espresso, cinnamon and milk. Mix the flour, baking soda, baking powder and salt into the egg mixture until well blended.

4. Fold in the crushed candy bars and chocolate chips.

5. Spoon the batter evenly into each muffin cup, about two-thirds full.

6. Sprinkle the reserved chopped candy over top of each muffin.

7. Bake 16 to 18 minutes, or until a toothpick inserted in the center of a muffin comes out clean. Makes 12 muffins.

Dove® Promises® Dark Chocolate Belgian Waffles

These always come out perfectly and are so-o-o delicious.

DIFFICULTY: 🍫🍫

EQUIPMENT: double boiler, wire whisk, Belgian waffle iron, electric mixer

FOR THE WAFFLES

14 Dove® Promises® Dark Chocolate
  Miniatures, unwrapped
2 egg yolks
2 cups buttermilk
2 tablespoons sugar
2 1/2 cups flour
1 teaspoon baking powder
1 teaspoon baking soda
1/2 cup unsweetened cocoa
1/2 teaspoon salt
3 egg whites

MAKE THE WAFFLES

1. In a double boiler, melt the chocolates over medium heat and stir until smooth. Separate the double boiler and set aside.

2. Preheat the waffle iron to medium. Spray with nonstick spray.

3. In a large bowl using a wire whisk, combine the egg yolks, buttermilk, sugar, flour, baking powder, baking soda, cocoa and salt, and beat until smooth. Stir in the melted chocolate.

4. In a separate clean, dry bowl using the electric mixer, beat the egg whites until stiff peaks form.

5. Fold the egg whites into batter until well combined.

6. Pour 1 cup of batter onto the waffle iron and cook for approximately 5 minutes, or until waffles are browned. Serve with warm maple or chocolate syrup. Makes 5 waffles.

DOVE® PROMISES®

Dove® candy debuted in 1992 and was the first dark chocolate produced by Mars. According to journalist Joël Glenn Brenner, the author of *The Emperors of Chocolate*, the beans for Dove® chocolate candies are a carefully guarded company secret.

The Mars Company had found a cocoa bean that was both rich in flavor and affordable enough to be used in inexpensive commercial candy. Top secret recipes, including secret cocoa beans, are an unwritten law in the hush-hush candy industry. It is a culture reminiscent of Roald Dahl's classic book *Charlie and the Chocolate Factory*.

WAFFLES

The ancient Greeks were the first to cook cake batter between two hot metal plates. They called their cakes *obelios*. In the thirteenth century, the plates were stamped to look like a honeycomb. These cakes came to be known as waffles, which came from an Old French term, *wafla*. Waffles were also a staple of French country cooking.

Sweet Holidays

~ *Seasonal Candy Bar Recipes* ~

Nestlé® White Crunch® 4th of July Trifle

~ *Our friends voted this recipe their favorite dessert in the book.* ~

DIFFICULTY: 🍫🍫

EQUIPMENT: deep serving bowl at least 10 x 6 inches (a clear bowl is especially nice), electric mixer

FOR THE FILLING

½ cup sugar
1 cup hot tap water
1 teaspoon vanilla
2 pints fresh blueberries
2 pints fresh raspberries or strawberries
2 bananas
5 Nestlé® White Crunch® Bars (1.4 oz. bars)
4 cups whipping cream
½ cup powdered sugar, sifted
1 box instant vanilla pudding (5.1 oz. box)
1 12- or 16-ounce frozen pound cake
½ cup blackberry or boysenberry syrup

FOR THE WHIPPED CREAM TOPPING

½ cup of whipping cream
1 tablespoon powdered sugar, sifted
¼ teaspoon vanilla

PREPARE THE COMPONENTS OF FILLING

1. Dipping Liquid: Combine the sugar, hot tap water and vanilla in a bowl, and mix together until dissolved.

2. Fruit Layer: Wash, drain, and pat dry the blueberries and raspberries or strawberries. (If using strawberries, slice berries into bite-sized pieces.) Set aside with the bananas. Reserve 5 of each berry for garnish.

3. White Crunch® Layer: Chop the candy bars into ¼-inch pieces. Set aside. Reserve 2 tablespoons for garnish.

4. Custard Cream Layer: In a large mixing bowl, combine the whipping cream and powdered sugar. Using electric mixer, mix for 30 seconds. Add the pudding mix and whip until the mixture forms stiff peaks. Refrigerate until ready to assemble.

5. Pound Cake Layer: Slice the whole pound cake into ½-inch slices.

ASSEMBLE THE TRIFLE

1. Using half of the sliced pound cake for the first layer, dip the pound cake slices into the dipping liquid and arrange in the bottom of the serving bowl.

2. Drizzle 1/4 cup of blackberry syrup over the pound cake slices.

3. Peel and slice one banana on top of the pound cake.

4. Sprinkle 1 pint each of blueberries and raspberries or strawberries on top of the sliced banana.

5. Sprinkle half of the chopped candy on top of the fruit.

6. Spread half of the custard cream mixture over the white chocolate.

7. With the remaining ingredients, repeat the layering process.

MAKE THE WHIPPED CREAM TOPPING

1. In a large mixing bowl, combine the cream, powdered sugar and vanilla. Beat until stiff peaks form.

2. Spread a thin layer of whipped cream evenly over top layer of custard.

3. Garnish with the reserved fruit and chopped candy. Serves 15 to 18.

NESTLÉ® WHITE CRUNCH®

According to company history, Henri Nestlé was a Swiss scientist and trained pharmacist in the 1860's. He developed a nutritional substitute for breast milk and also sold condensed milk. In the late 1800's his company merged with a company that made milk chocolate. Nestlé® Milk Chocolate Bar, with and without almonds, was introduced to America in 1919. Nestlé Crunch® appeared in 1938. Nestlé Alpine White® and White Crunch® were introduced in the 1980's.

Necco® Sweethearts® Cupcakes

∾ Our first conversation heart of the new millennium read Marry Me.
The rest goes without saying... ∾

DIFFICULTY: 🍫🍫
EQUIPMENT: muffin pan, paper baking cups, double boiler, electric mixer

FOR THE CHOCOLATE CUPCAKES

1 cup semi-sweet chocolate chips
1/3 cup milk
1 cup mayonnaise
2 cups sugar
4 eggs
1 teaspoon vanilla
2 cups flour
1 cup unsweetened cocoa
2 teaspoons baking soda
3/4 cup water

FOR THE VANILLA FROSTING

3 cups powdered sugar, sifted
1/3 cup butter, room temperature
1 teaspoon vanilla
2 tablespoons milk
1 box Sweethearts®

MAKE THE CUPCAKES

1. Preheat the oven to 350°. Line cupcake pans with paper baking cups.

2. In a double boiler over medium heat, melt the chocolate chips with the milk and stir until smooth. Separate the double boiler and let the chocolate cool for 5 minutes.

3. In a large bowl using electric mixer, cream together mayonnaise, sugar, eggs and vanilla.

4. Mix in the flour, cocoa, baking soda and water. Blend on medium, scraping down the sides of the bowl.

5. Add the chocolate mixture and incorporate thoroughly.

6. Pour the batter evenly into the paper-lined pans, filling each cup two-thirds full.

7. Bake for 17 to 19 minutes or until a toothpick inserted in the center of the cupcake comes out clean. Cool completely before frosting.

MAKE THE FROSTING

1. In a large bowl, cream together the powdered sugar and butter. Add the vanilla.

2. Gradually add the milk and beat until the frosting is spreadable.

3. Spread 2 tablespoons of frosting over each cupcake. Top with a Sweetheart®. Makes 30 cupcakes.

SWEETHEARTS® CONVERSATION HEARTS

Necco has made an impression on the hearts of Americans since 1866. According to company lore, the first sayings were printed on slips of paper and tucked inside candy scallop shells like fortune cookies. In 1902 they began to stamp the sayings on candy hearts. In those days the candy hearts were called Mottos®. Mottos® also came in other shapes, such as candy postcards, watches, baseballs and horseshoes. Six of the original Sweethearts® sayings are still in circulation: *Be Mine*, *Be True*, *My Man*, *Kiss Me*, *Sweet Talk*, and *Be Good*. Today, Necco pumps out 8 billion conversation hearts a year. At 33 cents a box, talk is still cheap.

Chocolate Easter Bunny Fondue

⤳ This "hare"-brained idea is a ton of fun. ⤳

DIFFICULTY: 🍫
EQUIPMENT: double boiler, fondue pot (optional), fondue forks or bamboo skewers

FOR THE FONDUE

16 ounces of chocolate Easter bunnies
²⁄₃ cup whipping cream
1 teaspoon orange extract (optional)

MAKE THE FONDUE

1. Prepare items for dipping and toppings.

2. In a double boiler over medium-low heat, melt the chocolate bunnies. Add ⅓ of the cream and orange extract. Stir until smooth.

3. Add the remaining cream and stir until thoroughly incorporated. Transfer to a fondue pot or serve from the double boiler.

4. Using fondue forks or bamboo skewers, dip the prepared items into the chocolate and roll them in the toppings. Serves 8 to 10.

Ideas for Dipping
Marshmallow Peeps®
Marshmallow Bunnies®
Pound cake, cut in bite-sized pieces
Mini pretzels
Brownies, cut in bite-sized pieces
Pineapple cubes
Strawberries
Sliced bananas
Sliced apples
Mandarin oranges

Ideas for Toppings
Heath® Bars, chopped
Butterfinger®, chopped
Whoppers®, chopped
Chopped nuts
Toasted coconut

MARSHMALLOW PEEPS®

The coolest chicks in America are Marshmallow Peeps®. These sugarcoated marshmallow chicken croquettes have been hatching steadily since 1953. Back then, according to Just Born Company lore, it took 27 hours to make one batch of Peeps®, because employees piped each hatchling by hand from a pastry bag. Even the eyes were meticulously hand-painted. Today Peeps® march off the line at a rate of 3,500 per minute. In perfectly aligned rows, the poker-faced chicks move in a backward parade toward waiting cardboard trays. When a visitor to the factory asked why they traveled backward, the worker replied, "Because if they knew where they were going, they'd run away!"

Christmas Wreath Cookies with Red Hots®

⚬ This recipe was a Christmas tradition at Ric's house. ⚬

DIFFICULTY: 🔸
EQUIPMENT: cookie sheet, plastic wrap

FOR THE WREATHS

4 ounces butter (1 stick)
40 marshmallows
1/2 teaspoon vanilla
1/2 teaspoon green food coloring, a few drops more or less depending on desired shade of green
5 cups corn flakes
54 Red Hots®

MAKE THE WREATHS

1. Wrap a cookie sheet in plastic wrap and set aside.

2. In a large saucepan over medium heat, melt the butter and marshmallows. Stir until smooth and remove from heat. Add the vanilla.

3. Stir in the food coloring until mixture becomes uniform in color.

4. Add the corn flakes and stir until well coated. Cool 5 minutes.

5. Fill a small dish with water for wetting fingers. Spoon 2-inch balls of the cereal mixture onto the prepared cookie sheet and shape into wreaths. (Dip fingers into water in between wreaths to prevent sticking.)

6. Decorate each wreath with 3 Red Hots® to look like red berries. Cool completely and store in an airtight container. Makes 15 to 18 wreaths.

HISTORY OF RED HOTS®

Ferrara Pan makes Red Hots®, Atomic Fireballs®, Boston Baked Beans® and other classic American candy. "Ferrara" stands for the founder's last name, and "Pan" stands for the unique panning process this company has used to make its candies since 1908.

A Red Hot® begins as a hard candy pellet. Thousands of pellets fill rows of steel pans that look like orbed kettledrums. Each pan has a wide, round opening like an industrial clothes dryer. These caldrons tilt at an angle to keep the candy from falling out as they rotate. Dippers filled with corn syrup are ladled into the whirling pans. This coats the pellets with a candy shell. As the pans turn, the candy gets bigger. Pails of sizzling red cinnamon flavor are also added. After the Red Hots® are buffed in polishing pans, they cascade into snack-sized boxes. The little boxes whiz by on belts and plunge neatly into bigger boxes for shipping.

Candy Cane Cheesecake with Chocolate Glaze

⌒ Deck the halls with a peppermint twist. ⌒

DIFFICULTY: ▲▲▲

EQUIPMENT: food processor fitted with a metal blade, 10-inch springform pan, aluminum foil, drinking glass (as needed), electric mixer, cookie sheet, double boiler

TO BEGIN, CRUSH THE CANDY CANES

8 candy canes (8 oz. total)

1. In the food processor, finely crush the candy canes.
2. Divide as follows into small bowls and set aside: 2 tablespoons for the crust, $^3/_4$ cup for the filling and 2 tablespoons for garnish.

FOR THE CRUST

35 OREO® Chocolate Sandwich Cookies
2 tablespoons crushed candy canes
4 tablespoons butter, melted
2 tablespoons water

FOR THE FILLING

24 ounces cream cheese
2 large eggs
1 cup sour cream
1 cup sugar
$^3/_4$ cup crushed candy canes
$^1/_2$ teaspoon peppermint extract

FOR THE GLAZE

1 cup semi-sweet chocolate chips
2 tablespoons butter
5 ounces whipping cream

MAKE THE CRUST

1. Preheat the oven to 375°. Wrap the bottom of a 10-inch springform pan with aluminum foil.
2. Finely crush the OREO® cookies in the food processor. Add 2 tablespoons of crushed candy canes and pulse 3 times.
3. With the food processor running, add the melted butter and water to the cookie crumbs, and process until well blended.

4. Transfer the cookie crumb mixture to the pan and press evenly over the bottom and halfway up the sides. The crust should be about $1/4$-inch thick.

5. Bake for 12 minutes. The crust may rise slightly during baking. Use the flat bottom of a drinking glass to gently press down the crust. Set aside.

6. Reduce the oven temperature to 350°.

MAKE THE FILLING

1. In a large bowl, using an electric mixer on medium, beat the cream cheese until light and fluffy.

2. Add eggs one at a time, scraping down the sides after each addition.

3. Mix in the sour cream and sugar, scraping down the sides.

4. Add $3/4$ cup crushed candy canes and peppermint extract. Mix well.

5. Pour the filling into the crust. Place the cheesecake on a cookie sheet and bake at 350° for about 1 hour and 15 minutes. The cheesecake will form a dome when it is fully baked.

6. Transfer to a rack and cool for 30 minutes.

7. Refrigerate for an hour before glazing.

(As cheesecake cools, the dome will fall, forming a shallow crater.)

MAKE THE CHOCOLATE GLAZE

1. In a double boiler over medium heat, melt chocolate chips and butter with $1/3$ of the cream. Remove from heat and stir until smooth. Stir in the remaining cream and mix until thoroughly incorporated.

GLAZE THE CHEESECAKE

1. Remove cake from refrigerator and run a knife around the edge of the pan to loosen the cheesecake. Release the cheesecake and place it on a serving plate.

2. Pour the glaze into the shallow crater and cover loosely with plastic wrap. Refrigerate for at least 10 minutes to allow the glaze to set.

3. Garnish with 2 tablespoons of crushed candy canes. Serves 12.

THE CANDY CANE LEGEND

The candy cane has its humble origins in the story of Christmas. As legend has it, the candy cane symbolizes the shepherd's staff. When turned upside down, another legend says the sugary stick stands for the initial "J," the first letter in the name Jesus. The white part of the candy cane symbolizes the purity of the Christ child. The red stripes symbolize the blood of Christ, or the sacrifice Jesus made for mankind.

Still another story is that of a choir conductor in Germany, who in 1670 gave the youngest members of his choir white candy sticks, shaped like a shepherd's crook, to keep them quiet during the long Christmas service. In the 1800's, a German-Swedish immigrant named August Imgard was thought to have brought the candy cane to America. In the 1920's, Bob McCormack was among the first Americans to make candy canes in the United States, hand-twisting them for family and friends. Today Bob's Candies are the largest producers of candy canes in the world.

Leftover Halloween Candy Cake

≈ For a Halloween treat, swirl your leftover candy into this sampler cake. ≈

DIFFICULTY: 🍫🍫
EQUIPMENT: 13 x 9-inch pan, electric mixer

FOR THE CAKE

12 Fun Size® candy bars (8-8.5 oz. total)
2 tablespoons milk
1 box white cake with pudding in the mix
  (18.5 oz. box)
1 cup water
$1/3$ cup vegetable oil
3 eggs
2 tablespoons flour

FOR THE FROSTING

$1/2$ cup unsweetened cocoa
$2^1/2$ cups powdered sugar, sifted
1 teaspoon vanilla
6 tablespoons butter, softened
3 tablespoons plus 2 teaspoons milk

MAKE THE CAKE

1. Preheat the oven to 350°. Lightly butter and flour a 13 x 9-inch cake pan.
2. In a medium saucepan over medium-low heat, melt the candy bars with the milk.
   Stir until the candy has melted. Cool for 5 minutes.
3. In a large bowl using an electric mixer, blend the cake mix, water, oil and eggs on low, scraping down the sides of the bowl. Beat for 2 minutes on high.
4. Stir $2/3$ cup of cake batter and the flour into the cooled chocolate mixture and mix until thoroughly incorporated.
5. Pour the remaining white cake batter into the prepared pan. Spoon the chocolate mixture on top of the cake batter. Swirl the chocolate mixture into the cake batter with a knife.
6. Bake for 28 to 32 minutes or until a toothpick inserted in the center of the cake comes out clean. Completely cool the cake in the pan before frosting.

MAKE THE FROSTING

1. In a large bowl using electric mixer, cream together the cocoa, powdered sugar, vanilla and butter on high. Gradually add the milk and beat until the frosting is spreadable. Frost the top of the cake. Serves 18-20.

Jolly Rancher® Christmas Tree Ornaments

*∽ Wrap these stained glass candy ornaments in
cellophane for a neat holiday gift. ∽*

DIFFICULTY: 🔻
EQUIPMENT: plastic straws, cookie cutters,
cookie sheet, pretty ribbon

FOR THE ORNAMENTS

*2 bags of Jolly Rancher® candies (7 oz. bags),
about 34 candies*

MAKE THE ORNAMENTS

1. Spray cookie sheet and selected cookie
   cutters with nonstick spray. Arrange cookie cutters on a cookie sheet. Set aside.

2. To make the holes for hanging ornaments, cut plastic straws into 2-inch
   pieces. Stand a piece of straw upright
   inside each cookie cutter where hole is
   desired.

3. Sort the Jolly Rancher® candies by color.

4. In a heavy saucepan over medium-low
   heat, melt the watermelon, cherry and a
   few of the grape candies.

5. In another saucepan over medium heat,
   melt the lemon and apple candies. Stir
   each until smooth.

6. Careful not to burn fingers, hold straws
   in place and pour melted candy into each
   cookie cutter. If necessary, press down
   lightly on the cookie cutters to prevent
   candy from leaking out the sides.

7. Cool for 10 minutes before removing
   cookie cutters and straws. When ornaments have cooled, insert a pretty piece
   of ribbon to hang each one. Makes 8 to
   10 ornaments.

JOLLY RANCHERS®

The original "jolly ranchers" were Bill and Dorothy Harmsen. This western couple owned and operated a
soft-serve ice cream and candy store in Golden, Colorado. In 1951, they sold their ice cream business and
turned their barn into a candy factory, known as the "Sugar Bar Ranch." They chose the name Jolly
Rancher® to give a friendly, Old West feel to their candies. One of their best-selling items was a hot cinnamon taffy stick, now known as Fire Stix®. They also created an assortment of fruit-flavored candy sticks.

Bit-O-Honey® Pumpkin Bars
with Cream Cheese Frosting
∽ A bit-o-heaven. ∽

DIFFICULTY: 🍫🍫
EQUIPMENT: 13 x 9-inch pan, food processor fitted with a metal blade, electric mixer

FOR THE PUMPKIN BARS

5 Bit-O-Honey® Bars (1.7 oz. bars)
1 cup canola oil
4 eggs
1 15-ounce can of pure pumpkin
1 cup sugar
2 teaspoons ground cinnamon
³/₄ teaspoon ground cloves
1 teaspoon ground allspice
¹/₄ teaspoon ground ginger
¹/₂ teaspoon ground nutmeg
¹/₄ teaspoon salt
2 teaspoons baking powder
1 teaspoon baking soda
2 cups flour

FOR THE CREAM CHEESE FROSTING

8 ounces cream cheese, room temperature
2 ounces butter (¹/₂ stick), room temperature
1 teaspoon vanilla
4 cups powdered sugar, sifted

MAKE THE PUMPKIN BARS

1. Preheat the oven to 350°. Spray a 13 x 9-inch pan with nonstick spray.

2. Freeze the Bit-O-Honey® bars for 10 minutes.

3. In the food processor, chop candy bars coarsely. Set aside.

4. In a large mixing bowl using electric mixer, combine the oil and eggs, and mix for 30 seconds on high. Add pumpkin, sugar, cinnamon, cloves, allspice, ginger, nutmeg and salt. Mix on medium for 1 minute, scraping down the sides of the bowl.

5. Add the baking powder, baking soda and flour, and mix on low for 30 seconds.

continued on next page

6. Fold in the chopped candy bars.

7. Pour the batter into the prepared pan and bake for 25 minutes, or until a toothpick inserted in the center of the cake comes out clean. Cool completely before frosting.

Make the Cream Cheese Frosting

1. In a large mixing bowl using electric mixer, beat together the cream cheese and butter until smooth and fluffy (about 3 minutes). Mix in the vanilla.

2. Add the powdered sugar and beat until thoroughly incorporated.

3. Spread the frosting evenly over the top of the cooled pumpkin bars. Cut into 2 x 3-inch squares. Makes 18-20 bars.

BIT-O-HONEY®

The Schutter-Johnson Company debuted Bit-O-Honey® in 1924. Bit-O-Honey® also had a companion bar called Bit-O-Coconut®. Still chewy to this day, Bit-O-Honey® is now manufactured by Nestlé.

Sticky Fingers

~ Recipes for Kids ~

Pop Rocks® Crispy Rice Bars
∽ A c-c-crackling c-c-combination. ∽

DIFFICULTY: 🍫
(needs adult supervision for using stove top)
EQUIPMENT: 13 x 9-inch pan, wooden spoon

4 ounces of butter (1 stick)
40 marshmallows
$\frac{1}{2}$ teaspoon vanilla
5 cups crisped rice cereal
12 bags Pop Rocks® candy (.33 oz. bags)

MAKE THE CRISPY RICE BARS

1. Spray a 13 x 9-inch pan with nonstick spray.

2. In a large saucepan over medium-low heat, melt the butter and marshmallows. Remove from heat.

3. Using a wooden spoon, stir in the vanilla and the crisped rice cereal until well coated.

4. Mix in the Pop Rocks® until fully incorporated.

5. Spread the mixture into the prepared 13 x 9 pan.

6. Cool completely before cutting and eating. Makes 18 noisy, 2 x 3-inch bars. Store in an airtight container.

POP ROCKS®

ChupaChups Candy Company introduced the crackling candy novelty Pop Rocks® to the American market in the 1970's. Urban myths abound regarding Pop Rocks®, including the one about Life® cereal's famous child spokesman Mikey, who supposedly overdosed and died while eating them—which, of course, has no truth to it whatsoever.

Candy Nachos

∾ As fun to make as they are to eat. ∾

DIFFICULTY: ♦♦
(needs adult supervision for using oven and electric mixer)
EQUIPMENT: paper towels, large serving plate, muffin pan, electric mixer

FOR THE NACHOS

4 ounces butter (1 stick), room temperature
1 1/2 cups powdered sugar, sifted
1 1/2 tablespoons corn syrup
3/4 cup all-purpose flour

FOR THE REFRIED BEANS

1 small box instant chocolate pudding (3.9 oz. box)

FOR THE GROUND MEAT

1 small bag Nestlé® buncha Crunch®

FOR THE LETTUCE, TOMATO AND PEPPERS

1 box Mike and Ike® candy
1 box Hot Tamales® candy (if you like it hot!)

FOR THE CHEESE

1 box Sno Caps®

MAKE THE NACHOS

1. Preheat oven to 350°. Lay a paper towel on a plate large enough to hold 12 nachos. Set aside.

2. In a medium bowl using electric mixer, cream the butter, sugar and corn syrup on high until pale and fluffy. Mix in the flour on low.

3. Place 1 level teaspoon of batter into the bottom of each muffin cup. (Do not use paper baking cups in the muffin pan.)

4. Bake until golden brown, about 6 to 7 minutes. Remove from oven and let sit for 2 minutes. Loosen the nachos with a knife and lift each one out of the muffin cup and set on the prepared plate. Cool completely and set aside. Repeat this process with the remaining dough. Makes 30 to 40 nachos.

continued on next page

Make the Refried Beans

1. Prepare the chocolate pudding as directed on the box.
2. Refrigerate for 5 minutes before assembling nachos.

Assemble the Nachos

1. Place 15 to 18 nachos on a serving plate.
2. Drop 1 cup of pudding in small amounts over the nachos.
3. Sprinkle buncha Crunch® over the pudding.
4. Scatter the Mike and Ike® and Hot Tamales® evenly over top of nachos.
5. Sprinkle with Sno-Caps®. Serve immediately. Makes 2 plates of Candy Nachos.

MIKE AND IKE® AND HOT TAMALES®

The Just Born Company has been producing Mike and Ike® and Hot Tamales® since 1953. Samuel Born, a Russian immigrant, founded his company in Brooklyn, New York. According to company history, the name Just Born came from the idea that Mr. Born's candy was thought to be so fresh, it was as if it had been just born! A baby doll cradled in a scale became the company's first emblem. Mr. Born was also a clever inventor who created the Born Sucker Machine, which automated the insertion of sticks into lollipops. He was also the father of Jimmies, the chocolate sprinkles that top ice cream cones. Over the years, the Born family business sold everything from fine chocolates packed in velvet-lined boxes to Marshmallow Peeps®.

Circus Peanuts Cereal

If you like cereal with marshmallow bits, then you'll go bananas for Circus Peanuts Cereal!

DIFFICULTY: ◣

EQUIPMENT: cereal bowl, scissors or knife

FOR THE CEREAL

3 circus peanuts candy marshmallow treats
1 ½ cups crisped rice cereal or oat rings cereal
1 cup milk

MAKE THE CEREAL

1. Pour a bowl of crisped rice cereal or oat rings cereal.
2. With a pair of clean scissors or a knife, cut the circus peanuts into ¼-inch square pieces.
3. Mix the circus peanuts and the cereal until well combined.
4. Add the milk. Makes one serving.

CIRCUS PEANUTS

Imagine brown paper sacks filled with puffed orange peanuts and a ringside seat for an elephant act under the big top on a summer's afternoon. These are some of the nostalgic images that circus peanuts bring to mind. Circus peanuts are descendents of the marshmallow, the fabled treat of the ancient Egyptian pharaohs. Manufactured in rows and rows of portly peanut-shaped molds since the 1800's, circus peanuts used to be sold only in springtime because they tended to harden with strong shifts in temperature. The Spangler Candy Co. in Ohio says the discovery of cellophane packaging in the 1940's allowed circus peanuts to become available year-round.

Candy Corn Peanut Chews

∾ *This is excellent junk food.* ∾

DIFFICULTY: 🍫🍫

(needs adult supervision for operating electric mixer, stove top and oven)
EQUIPMENT: 13 x 9-inch baking pan, electric mixer

FOR THE CAKE LAYER

1 box chocolate cake mix (18.25 oz. box)
1/2 cup butter, softened
1 egg
3 cups miniature marshmallows
1 cup chocolate chips

FOR THE TOPPING

1/2 cup corn syrup
1/4 cup sugar
1/4 cup brown sugar
1/2 cup peanut butter
1 teaspoon vanilla
2 cups crisped rice cereal
2 cups peanuts
1 cup candy corn
1 cup semi-sweet chocolate chips

MAKE THE CAKE LAYER

1. Preheat oven to 350°. Spray a 13 x 9-inch pan with nonstick spray.

2. In a large bowl using electric mixer, beat together the cake mix, butter and egg on low until well blended. Scrape the cake batter into the prepared pan, and spread evenly over the bottom. (The batter will be much thicker than normal cake batter.)

3. Bake for 12 to 16 minutes, or until a toothpick inserted in the center of the cake comes out clean.

4. Sprinkle mini-marshmallows evenly over the top of the cake as soon as cake is done.

5. Place the cake back into the oven for 3 minutes. Remove from oven and sprinkle chocolate chips evenly over the marshmallows. Set aside.

MAKE THE TOPPING

1. In a large saucepan over medium-high heat, combine the corn syrup, sugar and brown sugar. Heat to a boil, stirring

continued on next page

constantly. Remove from heat.

2. Add the peanut butter and vanilla, and mix until smooth.

3. Add the crisped rice cereal, peanuts, candy corn and the chocolate chips. Mix until all ingredients are well coated. Spread over the top of the cooled cake.

4. Allow topping to cool completely before cutting and serving. Makes 18 to 20 2 x 3-inch bars.

BRACH'S® CANDY CORN

Brach's Confections, founded in 1904, produces about 3.6 billion pieces of candy corn a year—the most in the world. If stacked end-to-end, their candy corn kernels would circle the earth two and a half times.

Candy corn originated in the Midwest and is still produced today almost entirely in the Chicago area. In the late 1880's farming was the biggest industry in the Midwest, and candy in the shape of a corn kernel was considered a novelty. We still associate candy corn with harvest time and Halloween.

Ants on a Log

DIFFICULTY: ◢

1 celery stalk
3 tablespoons peanut butter
12 Raisinets®

1. Wash and dry a celery stalk, trimming the ends.
2. Fill the trough of the celery stalk with peanut butter. Place the Raisinets® on top of the peanut butter. Cut into thirds or quarters. Makes 3 to 4 snacks.

Pigs in Blankets

DIFFICULTY: ◢

2 Fruit Roll-Ups®
2 large Tootsie Rolls® (2.25 oz. each)

1. Unroll a Fruit Roll-Up® and remove from plastic.
2. Unwrap a Tootsie Roll® and place it on one edge of the Fruit Roll-Up®.
3. Roll the Tootsie Roll® and the Fruit Roll-Up® together like a sleeping bag.
4. Repeat with the second Fruit Roll-Up®.

5. Cut into thirds and serve. Makes 6 snacks.

TOOTSIE ROLLS®

Leo Hirshfield began to make hand-rolled chocolate taffy in 1896. The recipe originated in his native Austria. He wrapped the bite-sized rolls individually and sold them for a penny in his New York City candy shop. He called them Tootsie Rolls®, after a nickname he had given his daughter, Clara. Today the Tootsie Roll® is said to taste the same as it did in 1896—and still costs a penny. Over 49 million Tootsie Rolls® roll off the line at Tootsie Industries per day.

TOOTSIE POPS®

The Tootsie Pop®, the first lollipop with a chewy center, debuted in 1931. The wrapper shows children at play. Once in a great while, a wrapper includes a picture of an Indian shooting a star. Finding an Indian wrapper is considered good luck. According to Tootsie Industries, this legend comes from a ghost story about an Indian chief who appears in a visitation to a candy maker and reveals the secret of how to get a soft center inside a lollipop.

Hershey's® Classic Caramels Popcorn Balls

∽ You don't have to be a kid to enjoy caramel popcorn. ∽

DIFFICULTY: 🌢

(adult supervision for microwave and using stove top)

EQUIPMENT: spatula, wire rack, cookie sheet

FOR THE POPCORN BALLS

6 cups popped popcorn
36 Hershey's® Classic Caramels, unwrapped

MAKE THE POPCORN BALLS

1. Pop popcorn and remove any unpopped kernels. Transfer the popcorn into a large bowl.

2. In a large saucepan over medium-low heat, melt the caramels.

3. Pour the melted caramel over the popcorn. Mix with a spatula until the popcorn is well coated.

4. With wet hands, form a popcorn ball, about 4 inches around.

5. Set wire rack over cookie sheet and transfer popcorn balls to the rack to cool completely. Makes 8 to 10 popcorn balls.

To store, wrap in plastic wrap.

CRACKER JACK®

In 1896 a salesman sampled a fresh batch of the Rueckheim brothers' latest popcorn creation. "That's a crackerjack!" he declared. The popular expression clicked and the Cracker Jack® brand was born. Cracker Jack® hit another home run in 1908 when the popular baseball song "Take Me Out to the Ball Game" debuted. The famous line "Buy me some peanuts and Cracker Jack" is familiar to generations of Americans. Toy animals, tops, puzzles and prizes were added to the mix in 1912. The Sailor Jack™ and Bingo™ wrapper appeared in 1918. The boy, according to company lore, was based on F. W. Rueckheim's grandson, Robert. Today Cracker Jack® is a classic part of snack food Americana.

Jolly Rancher® Angel Food Cake

If you could eat a rainbow, this is what it would taste like.

DIFFICULTY: 🔸

(adult supervision using oven and mixer)
EQUIPMENT: angel food cake pan, food processor fitted with metal blade, electric mixer

FOR THE CAKE

20 Jolly Rancher® candies
1 box white angel food cake mix (16 oz. box)
1 1/2 cups water

FOR THE FROSTING

1/2 teaspoon lemon zest, chopped
6 tablespoons butter, softened
5 cups powdered sugar, sifted
1 teaspoon lemon extract
2 tablespoons lemon juice

MAKE THE CAKE

1. Preheat the oven to 350°.
2. In the food processor, chop the Jolly Rancher® candies into small pieces. Set aside a teaspoon of chopped candy for a garnish.
3. In a large bowl using electric mixer, com-bine the cake mix and chopped candy and blend for 20 seconds on low. Add water and mix for 30 seconds on low.
4. Pour the batter into angel food cake pan and bake 35 to 40 minutes until cake is lightly golden on top.
5. Invert cake and cool for 45 minutes before removing from the pan.

MAKE THE FROSTING

1. In a clean, dry medium bowl using electric mixer, cream together butter, powdered sugar, lemon extract, lemon juice and lemon zest on high for 3 minutes.

FROST THE CAKE

1. Frost the top and sides of the angel food cake with the lemon frosting.
2. Garnish with 1 teaspoon of finely chopped Jolly Rancher® candies. Serves 10.

Here's your fresh hot pizza!

Shortbread Pizza with Candy Toppings

⌐ One cookie pizza to go—hold the Swedish Fish! ⌐

DIFFICULTY: ♦♦♦

(adult supervision for oven and electric mixer)
EQUIPMENT: floured surface for rolling, rolling pin, 9-inch round cake pan, double boiler, electric mixer

FOR THE CRUST

6 tablespoons butter, room temperature
$1/3$ cup sugar
1 egg
$1/4$ teaspoon vanilla
$1 1/2$ cups all-purpose flour
$1/8$ teaspoon salt
$1/2$ cup chocolate chips

FOR THE TOPPINGS

Lots of large gumdrops (red for pepperoni, white for onions, black for olives)

FOR GROUND MEAT

Nestlé® buncha Crunch® and Raisinets®

FOR CHEESE

$1/2$ cup white chocolate chips

MAKE THE CRUST

1. Using an electric mixer, cream the butter and sugar on low in a medium bowl.

2. Add the egg and vanilla and mix until fully incorporated.

3. Add the flour and salt and mix on low until dough forms.

4. Using hands, shape dough into a 4-inch round disk. Wrap the dough in plastic and refrigerate for at least an hour. (Dough will keep up to 2 weeks in the refrigerator or can be frozen for several months.)

5. Preheat the oven to 375°.

6. Remove dough from the refrigerator and divide into 2 equal parts. One at a time, work each piece of dough between hands to soften it.

7. On a well-floured surface, roll the dough into a 10-inch round, about $1/8$-inch thick.

8. Transfer the rolled dough to the cake pan and press into the bottom to look like a pizza crust. Using the tines of a

continued on next page

fork, poke holes in the bottom of the crust to prevent bubbles from forming.

9. Bake for 15 minutes or until crust is golden brown. Remove from oven.

10. Pour chocolate chips evenly over the bottom of the crust. Let the chips rest for 5 minutes and spread evenly around to look like sauce.

11. Cool in the pan for 20 minutes. Remove from pan and cool completely before assembling the pizza.

Top the Pizza

1. Slice a few red gum drops for pepperoni.

2. Slice the white and black gumdrops and cut a small circle out of the centers to form onion rings and olives.

3. Sprinkle buncha Crunch® and Raisinets® for ground meat.

4. In a double boiler over medium heat, melt the white chocolate chips. Remove from heat.

5. With a spoon drizzle the white chocolate over the toppings for melted cheese.

6. Cut into pizza slices. Serves 10 to 12.

Come up with your own candy pizza toppings, too!

A TRIP DOWN MEMORY LANE

This is a place to write down your favorite candy memories, candy recipes and candy rituals. Here's an idea to get you started:

If you have children, try planting Tootsie Pops® along the footpath to your front door on the first day of spring. Children can pick the candy flowers on their way home from school.

Top 3 Favorite Candy Bars _____

Favorite Candy Recipe _____

Favorite Candy to Give on Halloween _____

Favorite Movie Theater Candy _____

Favorite Candy to Receive on Valentine's Day _____

Favorite Super Bowl Candy _____

Favorite Easter Candy _____

Favorite Candy to Take on a Date _____

Favorite Candy Bar Memory _____

Favorite Candy Bar Tradition _____

Favorite Candy Novelty _____

Favorite Candy Bar Urban Myth _____

Favorite Candy Ritual _____

CANDY BAR RESOURCES

BOOKS

The Great American Candy Bar Book by Ray Broekel (Houghton Mifflin, 1982)

The Emperors of Chocolate: Inside the Secret World of Hershey and Mars by Joël Glenn Brenner (Alfred A. Knopf, 1999)

WEB SITES

National Confectioners Association: www.candyusa.org

Hershey's Foods Corporation: www.hersheys.com

M&M/Mars: www.m-ms.com

Jet-Puffed: www.jetpuffed.com

Tootsie Roll Industries: www.tootsie.com

Necco (New England Confectionery Co.): www.necco.com

Brown & Haley: www.brown-haley.com

Just Born: www.marshmallowpeeps.com

Scharffenberger: www.scharffen-berger.com

Nostalgic/Old-Fashioned Candy: www.californiacandy.com

Nestlé: www.NestleUSA.com

Ghirardelli: www.ghirardelli.com

Spangler Candy Co.: www.spanglercandy.com

Ferrara Pan Candy Co.: www.ferrarapan.com

Goetz: www.goetzcandy.com

ChupaChup:s www.chupachups.com

∽ *About the Authors* ∽

ALISON INCHES

Alison Inches has always loved candy and pop culture Americana. Her top 3 favorite candies are Peanut M&M's®, Dots® and Snickers®. Alison is the author of over 30 books for children, including the best-selling *Go to Bed, Fred* (Workman Publishing). She is also the author of 2 adult trade books, *In the Kitchen with Miss Piggy* (Time-Life) and a biography, *Jim Henson's Designs and Doodles* (Harry Abrams Publishers). If Alison had it her way, she would live in a gingerbread house with a Hershey® Bar front door, a Necco® Wafer path and an M&M's® patio. For now she lives with her husband Ric in Mountain View, California.

RIC MCKOWN

Ric is a graduate of the California Culinary Academy with a certificate in pastry and baking. His interest in cooking began when he was a boy. Back then, Ric's father was in research and development at General Mills and he often brought home new cereals to share with the family. Ric became an unofficial taste-tester, helping to bring such cereals as Golden Grahams® to market. Today, Ric owns Countrymade, a bakery based in Mountain View, California. He also works for a high-tech company in Silicon Valley. His top 3 favorite candy bars are Skor®, Nutrageous® and Junior Mints®. He loves volleyball, inline hockey, playing the guitar and spending time with his sweetheart, Alison.

GORDON KELLY